# Culinary Calculations

# Culinary Calculations

## Simplified Math for Culinary Professionals

TERRI JONES

WILEY
John Wiley & Sons, Inc.

This book is printed on acid-free paper. ∞



Published by John Wiley & Sons, Inc., Hoboken, New Jersey
Published simultaneously in Canada



For general information on our other products and services or for technical support, please contact our Customer Care Department within the United States at (800) 762-2974, outside the United States at (317) 572-3993 or fax (317) 572-4002.

Wiley also publishes its books in a variety of electronic formats. Some content that appears in print may not be available in electronic books. For more information about Wiley products, visit our web site at www.wiley.com.

***Library of Congress Cataloging-in-Publication Data:***

Jones, Terri,
Culinary calculations : simplified math for culinary professionals
/ by Terri Jones.
p. cm.
ISBN 0-471-22626-2 (Cloth)
1. Food service—Mathematics. I. Title.
TX911.3.M33J56 2003
647.95′01′51—dc21

Printed in the United States of America

10 9 8 7 6 5 4 3 2 1

# CONTENTS

# PREFACE

People who run successful food service operations understand that basic mathematics is necessary to accurately arrive at a plate cost (cost per guest meal) and to price a menu. Mathematics for food service is relatively simple. Addition, subtraction, multiplication, and division are the basic mathematical functions that must be understood. A calculator can assist with the accuracy of the calculations as long as you understand the reason behind the math. A simple computer spreadsheet or a more complex inventory and purchasing software package can also be used, but the underlying mathematics are still necessary to understand the information the computer programs are calculating.

Commercial food service operations are *for-profit* businesses. They are open to the public. Many commercial food service operations go out of business within the first five years of opening. The reasons for their demise are many. Some of the more common reasons for failure are cash-flow issues relating to incorrect recipe costing or incorrect portion controls. These mistakes, which are fatal, are often caused by simple mistakes in basic mathematics.

Take the example of the room chef at a busy hotel restaurant. One menu item was a wonderful fresh fruit salad priced at $4.95. When the Food and Beverage Cost Control Department added together the cost of all of the ingredients in one portion, the total cost was $4.85.

$4.95 (menu price) − $4.85 (plate cost) = $0.10 (items gross profit)

The gross profit on the item was only $0.10. For every fresh fruit salad sold, money was lost. Once the information on the plate cost was told to the chef, he adjusted the recipe to decrease the portion cost. The food and beverage director never found out.

The other day, I was having lunch with a woman who had recently taken over a small deli inside of a busy salon. After two months in operation, it occurred to her that she was losing money. In a panic, she decided to lower her menu prices. I asked her why she made that decision. She said it seemed like a good idea at the time. "Do you want to lose more money?" I asked. "If you are already losing money and you sell your products for less, you will end up losing more money."

$5.95 (old menu price) − $5.45 (new menu price)
= $0.50 (increased loss per sale)

A sandwich sold for $5.95. The new menu price is $5.45. The difference is $0.50. Now each time she sells a sandwich, her loss is increased by $0.50.

As the conversation progressed, the woman confessed that she had no idea what her food cost was per item. She had no idea if any of the menu items could produce a profit. She works full-time, so she hired employees to operate the business for her. She had no system of tracking sales. She had no idea if her employees were honest. How long do you think she can remain in business while losing money daily?

Noncommercial food service operations are *nonprofit* or *controlled-profit* operations. They are restricted to a certain population group. For example, the cafeteria at your school is only open and available to students and teachers at the school. Operating in a nonprofit environment means that costs must equal revenues. In this environment, accurate meal costs and menu prices are just as critical as they are in a for-profit business.

A number of years ago, the State of Arizona figured out the total cost to feed its prison population for one year. Unfortunately for the state budget, the cost per meal was off by $0.10. Ten cents is not a lot of money, and most of us are not going to be concerned with $0.10. However, prisoners eat 3 meals a day, 365 days a year. Ten million meals were served to the 9,133 prisoners that year. A $0.10 error became a million-dollar cost overrun.

9,133 (prisoners) × 3 (meals per day)
= 27,399 (meals served per day)

27,399 (meals served per day) × 365 (days in one year)
= 10,000,635 (total meals served annually)

10,000,000 (meals served annually, rounded) × $0.10 (10 cents)
= $1,000,000.00

The State of Arizona had to find an additional $1,000,000 that year to feed its prison population. That meant other state programs had to be cut or state tax rates needed to be raised.

These examples bring to light just how important basic mathematics are for successful food service operations. Accurate plate cost is critical regardless of the type of operation, the market it serves, or the profit motive. This text will assist you in learning how to use simple mathematics to run a successful food service operation.

## ACKNOWLEDGMENTS

Special thanks to my family for all of their support. Thanks to the culinary faculty and staff at CCSN for all of their help.

Thanks go to the reviewers of the manuscript for their valuable input. They are: G. Michael Harris, Bethune-Cookman College, Vijay S. Joshi, Virginia Intermont College, Nancy J. Osborne, Alaska Vocational Technical Center, Reuel J. Smith, Austin Community College

Finally, JoAnna Turtletaub, Karen Liquornik, Mary Kay Yearin, and Julie Kerr of John Wiley & Sons supported me from concept to publication. Thank you!

# Culinary Calculations

# Chapter 1
# INTRODUCTION TO BASIC MATHEMATICS

## BASIC MATHEMATICS 101: WHOLE NUMBERS

Mathematical concepts are necessary to accurately determine a cost per portion or plate cost. As we adjust our way of thinking about mathematics, we can begin to utilize it as a tool to ensure that we can run a successful food service operation. Correct mathematical calculations are the key to success. Let's review those basic mathematical calculations using a *midscale food service* operation. A midscale food service operation is a restaurant that serves three meal periods: breakfast, lunch, and dinner. It has affordable menu prices. The menu prices, or the *average guest check*, range from $5.00 to $10.00.

### Addition

A basic mathematical operation is addition. The symbol is +. Addition is the combining of two or more numbers to arrive at a sum. For example, a midscale restaurant serves three meal periods. If 80 customers are served breakfast, 120 are served lunch, and 150 are served dinner, how many customers have we served today?

| | |
|---|---|
| Breakfast: | 80 |
| Lunch: | 120 |
| Dinner: | +150 |
| Total customers served: | 350 |

## Subtraction

Subtraction is another basic mathematical operation. The symbol is −. Subtraction is the taking away or deduction of one number from another. Let's suppose that when we reviewed the number of meals served at our midscale restaurant, we found an error. We served only 70 customers at breakfast, not 80. When we adjust our customer count, we subtract:

| | |
|---|---|
| Original count: | 80 |
| Updated count: | − 70 |
| Difference: | 10 |

Now we can adjust our total customer count for the day by 10:

| | |
|---|---|
| Total customers served originally: | 350 |
| Adjustment for miscount: | − 10 |
| Updated customer count: | 340 |

## Multiplication

Multiplication is the mathematical operation that adds a number to itself a certain number of times to arrive at a *product.* It abbreviates the process of repeated addition. The symbol for multiplication is ×. For example, the 70 customers who ate breakfast had a choice of two entree items. One entree item uses two eggs and one uses three eggs. If 30 customers ordered the two-egg entree and 40 customers ordered the three-egg entree, how many eggs did we use?

$$30 \text{ customers} \times 2 \text{ eggs} = 60 \text{ eggs}$$

$$40 \text{ customers} \times 3 \text{ eggs} = 120 \text{ eggs}$$

To arrive at the total eggs used we add:

| | |
|---|---|
| | 60 eggs |
| | + 120 eggs |
| Total eggs used: | 180 |

## Division

Division is the mathematical operation that is the process of finding out how many of one number is contained in another. The answer is called a *quotient.* There are several symbols that represent division. They are ÷, /, $\frac{x}{y}$ or $\overline{)\ }$. Let's continue with the number of eggs we used during breakfast. We multiplied to figure out the total number of eggs we used for each entree item. Then we added the number of eggs used for each entree to arrive at the total used for breakfast.

Now let's figure out how many dozen eggs we used at breakfast. We know that there are 12 eggs per dozen. We need to divide the total eggs used by 12 (one dozen) to arrive at the number of dozen of eggs used.

180 eggs / 12 (number of eggs per dozen) = 15 dozen

We used 15 dozen eggs serving breakfast to 70 customers.

Continue with our basic mathematical operations and the breakfast meal period. We have a menu with our two entree items, we have the recipes for the entree items, and we have the purchasing unit of measure and cost. Division is often used to find one of something, as in cost per item. That is how it will be used here.

## BASIC MATHEMATICS 101: MENU, RECIPES, AND PURCHASING INFORMATION

### Basic Mathematics Menu

*Breakfast*

| | |
|---|---|
| Two eggs, any style | Three-egg omelette |
| Hash-brown potatoes | Hash-brown potatoes |
| Toast | Toast |
| $2.95 | $3.95 |

*Basic Mathematics Recipes*

| | |
|---|---|
| Two eggs, any style—2 eggs | Three-egg omelette—3 eggs |
| 4 oz. hash browns | 4 oz. hash browns |
| 2 slices bread | 2 slices bread |

### Purchasing Information

Eggs are purchased by the half case.
There are 15 dozen eggs per half case.
Cost per half case is $18.00.

Hash browns are purchased by the 5-pound bag.
A 5-pound bag costs $4.00.

Bread is purchased by the 2-pound loaf.
There are 20 slices in a standard loaf.
A 2-pound loaf costs $2.00.

How much does it cost for us to serve the entree items on our menu? We use our basic mathematical functions to arrive at the cost per portion, or plate cost. There are three items on each plate. The first item is the egg.

Eggs are purchased by the half case. There are 15 dozen eggs in a half case. There are 12 eggs per dozen. Our cost for 15 dozen is \$18.00. Here we divide the price per half case by the number of dozen eggs to find the cost per dozen.

\$18.00 / 15 dozen = \$1.20 per dozen eggs

Now that we have the cost per dozen eggs, we need to divide the cost per dozen eggs by 12 to find the cost per egg.

\$ 1.20 / 12 (eggs per dozen) = \$0.10 per egg

One egg costs \$0.10. Now we use multiplication to find out how much it costs for the eggs in our breakfast entrees. For the breakfast entree that uses two eggs:

\$0.10 (price per egg) × 2 (eggs) = \$0.20 (price for 2 eggs)

For the breakfast entree that uses three eggs:

\$0.10 (price per egg) × 3 (eggs) = \$0.30 (price for 3 eggs)

The total cost for the eggs used in the two-egg entree is \$0.20. The total cost for the eggs for the three-egg entree is \$0.30.

The next item on the plate is the hash browns. Hash browns are purchased by the 5-pound bag. A 5-pound bag costs \$4.00. We need to find the cost per pound. To do this we divide the \$4.00 by 5 pounds.

\$4.00 (cost for 5 pounds) / 5 (pounds per bag) = \$0.80 (cost per pound)

Then we need to find the cost per ounce. We know there are 16 ounces in 1 pound. We divide the cost per pound by 16 (number of ounces in a pound).

\$0.80 (cost per pound) / 16 (number of ounces in a pound) = \$0.05 (cost per ounce)

Hash browns cost \$0.05 per ounce. Our recipe uses 4 ounces of hash browns. We need to multiply the cost per ounce by the number of ounces in the recipe to determine the hash-brown portion cost on the plate we serve to the guest.

\$0.05 (cost per ounce) × 4 (number of ounces per portion) = \$0.20 (cost per portion)

The portion cost for hash browns on each entree plate is \$0.20.

Our last recipe item is the toast. A 2-pound loaf of bread costs \$2.00. There are 20 slices of bread in a standard 2-pound loaf. We need to find the cost per slice of bread.

$2.00 (cost per loaf) / 20 (number of slices)
= $0.10 (cost per slice of bread)

A slice of bread costs $0.10. We use 2 slices of bread. We need to multiply the cost per slice by the number of slices we use to determine our portion cost per entree.

$0.10 (cost per slice) × 2 (portion size)
= $0.20 (cost for 2 slices of toast)

The portion cost for the toast per entree is $0.20.

Now we can add together all of our ingredient costs to determine the total cost to serve one portion of each breakfast entree item. Let's start with the two-egg breakfast:

| | |
|---|---|
| Cost for 2 eggs: | $0.20 |
| Cost for 4 ounces of hash browns: | $0.20 |
| Cost for 2 slices of toast: | +$0.20 |
| Total cost to serve breakfast with 2 eggs: | $0.60 |

We served 30 customers the two-egg breakfast. How much did it cost to serve 30 portions?

30 (number of customers served) × $0.60 (cost for the entree)
= $18.00 (total cost for 30 portions)

The two-egg breakfast sells for $2.95. We sold 30 portions, so how much sales revenue did we collect?

30 (number of customers served) × $2.95 (menu price)
= $88.50 (sales revenue from 30 entrees)

What is our gross profit for the two-egg breakfast?

$88.50 (sales revenue from 30 entrees)
− $18.00 (total cost for 30 portions) = $70.50 (gross profit)

| | |
|---|---|
| Total sales 2 eggs: | $88.50 |
| Total cost of sales: | $18.00 |
| Gross profit: | $70.50 |

The three-egg breakfast is calculated in the same way. First, we add together all of the ingredient costs:

| | |
|---|---|
| Cost for 3 eggs: | $0.30 |
| Cost for 4 ounces of hash browns: | $0.20 |
| Cost for 2 slices of toast: | +$0.20 |
| Total cost to serve breakfast with 3 eggs: | $0.70 |

We served 40 customers the three-egg breakfast. How much did it cost to serve 40 portions?

40 (number of customers served) × \$0.70 (cost for the entree)
= \$28.00 (total cost for 40 portions)

The three-egg breakfast sells for \$3.95. If we sell 40 portions, how much sales revenue did we collect?

40 (number of entrees served) × \$3.95 (menu price)
= \$158.00 (sales revenue from 40 entrees)

What is our gross profit for the three-egg breakfast?

\$158.00 (total sales revenue) − \$28.00 (total cost for 40 portions)
= \$130.00 (gross profit)

| | |
|---|---|
| Total sales 3 eggs: | \$158.00 |
| Total cost of sales: | \$28.00 |
| Gross profit: | \$130.00 |

The total cost to serve 70 customers breakfast is:

\$18.00 (2-egg breakfast) + \$28.00 (3-egg breakfast)
= \$46.00 (total cost for breakfast served)

The total sales revenue collected from selling 70 customers breakfast is:

\$88.50 (2-egg breakfast) + \$158.00 (3-egg breakfast)
= \$246.50 (total sales revenue collected)

What is our total gross profit for breakfast?

\$246.50 (total sales revenue) − \$46.00 (total cost for breakfast)
= \$200.50 (total gross profit)

| | |
|---|---|
| Total sales breakfast: | \$246.50 |
| Total cost of sales: | \$46.00 |
| Total gross profit: | \$200.50 |

A profitable business operation is impossible without a solid understanding of mathematics. Addition, subtraction, multiplication, and division are the basic mathematical functions necessary for all food service calculations.

## BASIC MATHEMATICS 101: WHOLE-NUMBERS REVIEW PROBLEMS

Use this information to solve the problems that follow.

**Basic Mathematics 101: Review Menu**

| | |
|---|---|
| Chicken Fingers<br>French Fries<br>$6.95 | Cheeseburger<br>Onion Rings<br>$4.95 |

**Basic Mathematics 101: Review Recipes**

| | |
|---|---|
| 8 oz. chicken fingers | ¼ lb. hamburger patty<br>1 slice American cheese<br>1 hamburger bun |
| 3 oz. french fries | 3 oz. onion rings |

**Basic Mathematics 101:**
**Review Menu Purchasing Information**

Chicken fingers are purchased by the case.
A case weighs 10 pounds.
A case costs $25.00.

French fries are purchased by the case.
A case weighs 20 pounds.
A case costs $10.00.

Hamburger patties are purchased by the case.
A case weighs 20 pounds, patties are ¼ pound.
A case costs $30.00.

American cheese, sliced, is purchased by the case. A case has four 5-pound blocks.
Each block contains 80 slices of cheese.
Each case contains 320 slices of cheese.
A case costs $22.20.

Hamburger buns are purchased by the bag.
There are 12 hamburger buns per bag.
A bag costs $1.20.

Onion rings are purchased by the case.
A case weighs 15 pounds.
A case costs $11.25.

**1.** What is the cost for 1 pound of chicken fingers?

**2.** What is the cost for an 8-ounce portion of chicken fingers?

3. What is the cost for 1 pound of french fries?

4. What is the cost for a 3-ounce portion of french fries?

5. What is the plate or portion cost for the chicken-finger entree?

6. What is the gross profit per sale?

7. If we sell 185 chicken-finger entrees, what is the total sales revenue?

8. If we sell 185 chicken-finger entrees, what is the total product cost?

9. If we sell 185 chicken-finger entrees, what is the total gross profit?

10. What is the cost for a quarter-pound hamburger patty?

11. What is the cost for a slice of cheese?

12. What is the cost for a hamburger bun?

13. What is the cost for a pound of onion rings?

**14.** What is the cost for a 3-ounce serving of onion rings?

**15.** What is the plate or portion cost for the cheeseburger entree?

**16.** What is the gross profit per sale?

**17.** If we sell 225 cheeseburger entrees, what is the total sales revenue?

**18.** If we sell 225 cheeseburger entrees, what is the total product cost?

**19.** If we sell 225 cheeseburger entrees, what is the total gross profit?

**20.** What is our total sales revenue from the chicken fingers and cheeseburger entrees?

**21.** What is our total product cost from the chicken-finger and cheeseburger entree sales?

**22.** What is the total gross profit for our total sales?

### Basic Mathematics 101: Whole-Number Review Answers

1. Cost/weight: $2.50 per pound
2. Pound cost/16 (ounces per pound) × 8, or pound cost/2, $1.25 per 8-ounce portion
3. Cost/weight, $0.50 per pound
4. Pound cost/16 (ounces per pound) × 3, $0.0938, rounded to $0.09
5. Portion cost + portion cost, $1.34
6. Menu price − total portion or plate cost, $5.61
7. Total sales × menu price, $1,285.75
8. Total number sold × plate cost, $247.90
9. Total revenue − total cost, $1,037.85
10. Case weight/patty weight, 80 patties per case, then cost/number of patties, $0.375 per patty *or* cost /weight, $1.50 per pound then /4, $0.375 rounded to $0.38
11. Cost/total slices, $0.0694 rounded to $0.07
12. Cost/total buns, $0.10
13. Cost/weight, $0.75
14. Pound cost/16 (ounces per pound) × 3, $0.1406 rounded to $0.14
15. Portion cost pattie + portion cost bun + portion cost cheese + portion cost rings, $0.69
16. Menu price − total portion or plate cost, $4.26
17. Total sales × menu price, $1,113.75
18. Total number sold × plate cost, $155.25
19. Total revenue − total cost, $958.50
20. Total revenue chicken + total revenue cheeseburger, $2,399.50
21. Total + total cost, $403.15
22. Total revenue − total cost, $1,996.35.

## BASIC MATHEMATICS 102: MIXED NUMBERS AND NONINTEGERS QUANTITIES

Mixed numbers are numbers that contain a whole number and a noninteger quantity, a *fraction.* Three and one half (3½) is a mixed number. All fractions, decimals, and/or percentages represent noninteger quantities. Basic mathematical operations apply to mixed numbers, fractions, decimals, and percentages. Noninteger quantities are common in food service mathematics.

## Fractions, Decimals, and Percentages

Any product purchased that is trimmed before cooking, or that "shrinks" during the cooking or portioning process, becomes a fraction, decimal, or percentage of the original purchase weight. Any time a guest is served a portion of a completed recipe, the guest is served a fraction, decimal, or percentage of the recipe yield.

Fractions, decimals, and percentages are different styles for representing a noninteger quantity. A common example of noninteger quantities is the system we use for monetary exchange in the United States. It is based on the decimal system. The decimal system expresses numbers in tens, multiples of ten, tenths and submultiples of ten. Decimals can easily be converted to fractions and/or percentages.

| *Unit* | *Decimal* | *Fraction* | *Percentage* |
|---|---|---|---|
| One dollar: | $1.00 | 1/1 | 100% |
| Half dollar: | $0.50 | 1/2 | 50% |
| Quarter: | $0.25 | 1/4 | 25% |
| Dime: | $0.10 | 1/10 | 10% |
| Nickel | $0.05 | 1/20 | .05% |
| Penny: | $0.01 | 1/100 | .01% |

The slicing of a whole pizza is based on fractions. A fraction is a noninteger quantity expressed in terms of a numerator and a denominator. Fractions can easily be converted into decimals and/or percentages.

**FIGURE 1.1** U.S. money.
Photography by Thomas Myers.

**FIGURE 1.2** Pizza sliced.
Photography by Thomas Myers.

| *Pizza* | *Fraction* | *Decimal* | *Percentage* |
|---|---|---|---|
| The whole pizza pie | 1/1 | 1.00 | 100% |
| We slice it down the center: | 1/2 | .50 | 50% |
| We slice each half (1/2) in half (1/2): | 1/2 × 1/2 = 1/4 | .25 | 25% |
| We slice each quarter (1/4) in half (1/2) | 1/4 × 1/2 = 1/8 | .125 | 12.5% |

We have divided our pizza into eight slices. Each slice is 1/8, .125, or 12.5 percent of the whole pie.

The conversion of a fraction to a decimal is achieved by dividing the denominator into the numerator and inserting the decimal point in the correct location (e.g., 1/8 = 1 ÷ 8, or .125). The conversion of a decimal to a percentage is achieved by multiplying the decimal by 100 and placing a percent sign to the right of the last digit (e.g., .125 × 100 = 12.5%). Note that when you multiply the decimal by 100, you just have to move the decimal point two places to the right.

Here is a less clear-cut example. We purchase broccoli, whole, by the pound. After the broccoli is received and before we serve it to our guests, we cut off the stem. As we cut the stem, we are cutting away some of the purchased weight. What we are left with is a fraction, decimal, or percentage of the original purchase weight.

If we purchase 1 pound of broccoli, whole, how much broccoli flowerettes can we serve?

The yield on a pound of broccoli, whole, is 62.8%. That means that 62.8% of the 16 ounces we purchased can be served as flowerettes. The mathematical operation that we use to find a part of something is multiplication. In this example, we multiply 16 ounces by the appropriate percentage, 62.8 percent.

**FIGURE 1.3** Broccoli from stem flowerettes.
Photography by Thomas Myers.

$$16 \text{ ounces} \times 62.8\% = 10 \text{ ounces}$$

The percentage, 62.8%, can be converted into a decimal by moving the decimal point two spaces to the left. The decimal equivalent of 62.8 percent is .628.

$$16 \text{ ounces} \times .628 = 10 \text{ ounces}$$

The percentage 62.8 percent can also be converted into a fraction by placing the 62.8 as a numerator and 100 as a denominator.

$$\frac{62.8}{100} \times \frac{16}{1} \text{(ounces)} = \frac{1.005}{100} \qquad \frac{1.005}{100} = 10 \text{ ounces}$$

Note that however you choose to do the multiplication, the result is the same: we can serve 10 ounces of broccoli flowerettes.

Now let's look at fractions as they pertain to portions of a larger recipe. A recipe for clam chowder produces a gallon of soup. One gallon of soup is equal to 128 ounces. If we serve an 8-ounce portion of clam chowder, the 8 ounces represents a fraction, decimal, or percentage of the total recipe yield.

As a fraction, the 8-ounce portion is the numerator and the 128 ounces is the denominator. Sometimes it is helpful to reduce the fraction to its lowest common denominator. This means the numerator and the denominator are divided by the same number in order to make the fraction user-friendly. (This is covered in more detail later in this chapter.)

$$\frac{8}{128} = \frac{8 / 8}{128 / 8} = \frac{1}{16}$$

To arrive at the decimal equivalent, we divide the numerator by the denominator. The decimal equivalent is .625.

$$\frac{1}{16} = 1 / 16 = .0625$$

To arrive at the percentage equivalent, we multiply the decimal by 100 (move the decimal two spaces to the right) and add the percentage sign to the right of the last digit.

$$\frac{1}{16} = .0625 \times 100 = 6.25\%$$

This means we can serve sixteen 8-ounce portions from this clam-chowder recipe.

If the cost for the entire recipe is $4.00, how much is one 8-ounce portion? We can multiply by the noninteger numbers we developed above. Whenever we multiply a whole number by a noninteger number that is less than 1, the product will always be less than the original whole number. This is because we are looking for a part of the original whole number. In this example, the cost for an 8-ounce portion (a part of the whole) of clam chowder will be less than $4.00 (the whole).

We can multiply by the fraction:

$$\$4.00 \text{ (cost for recipe)} \times \frac{1}{16} = \frac{\$4.00}{16} = \$0.25$$

We can multiply by the decimal equivalent:

$$\$4.00 \times .0625 = \$0.25$$

We can multiply by the percentage equivalent:

$$\$4.00 \times 6.25\% = \$0.25$$

The cost for an 8-ounce portion of clam chowder is $0.25. Twenty-five cents ($0.25) is 1/16 of $4.00, the cost for the entire recipe.

We can also use division to determine the cost per ounce and then use multiplication to determine the cost for an 8-ounce portion. The total recipe yield can be divided into the total recipe cost to determine the cost per ounce. Then the per-ounce cost can be multiplied by 8, the number of ounces.

$4.00 (cost for recipe) / 128 (total ounces in recipe)
= $0.03125 per ounce

Then we multiply the cost per ounce by 8.

$0.03125 (cost per ounce) × 8 (ounces in 1 portion) = $0.25

The result is the same: the cost for an 8-ounce portion of clam chowder is $0.25.

## Basic Mathematical Operations Using Fractions

Fractions are numbers that are expressed as a numerator over a denominator. A proper fraction is a number less than one (<1). The fraction for one half is $\frac{1}{2}$. The number 1 is the numerator and the number 2 is the denominator. An improper fraction is a number greater than one (>1). The fraction for the number 2 is $\frac{2}{1}$. The number 2 is the numerator and the number 1 is the denominator. There are special rules that apply to basic mathematical operations with fractions.

It is customary that proper fractions are reduced to their lowest terms after the mathematical operation is complete. Reducing a fraction to its lowest terms means that the greatest common factor of the numerator and the denominator is 1. Reducing a fraction to its lowest term is done by dividing both the numerator and the denominator by the greatest common factor that will divide evenly into both.

It is also customary that an improper fraction is reduced to a mixed number. An improper fraction has a numerator that is equal to or greater than the denominator. The process for reducing an improper fraction to a mixed number is to divide the denominator into the numerator.

**Addition with Fractions** Addition with fractions is a relatively simple process. The key is for all of the fractions in the equation to have a common denominator. Let's use the example of a pizza cut into eight slices. If you eat four slices, you have eaten:

$$\frac{1}{8} + \frac{1}{8} + \frac{1}{8} + \frac{1}{8} = \frac{4}{8}$$

Four-eighths (4/8) should be reduced to its lowest terms. This reduction is completed by using division. The key to reducing the fraction to its lowest term is to find the largest number that can be divided equally into both the numerator and the denominator. In the example of $\frac{4}{8}$, the number 2 and the number 4 can be divided equally into the numerator and the denominator. If we divide by the number 2:

$$\frac{4}{8} = \frac{4/2}{8/2} = \frac{2}{4}$$

our fraction is now $\frac{2}{4}$. This, however, is not the lowest term for this fraction because there is another number that can be divided evenly into the numerator and the denominator. When we divide by the number 4:

$$\frac{4}{8} = \frac{4/4}{8/4} = \frac{1}{2}$$

our fraction is now $\frac{1}{2}$. One-half ($\frac{1}{2}$) is equal to four-eighths ($\frac{4}{8}$), and it is the lowest term for this fraction.

When we add fractions that have the same denominator, we add the numerators together and use the denominator as is. When we have completed the addition process, the sum is reduced to the lowest term.

Every fraction will not have the same denominator. We may have to add two or more fractions together that do not have the same denominator. The first step in this situation is to find a common denominator. A *common denominator* is a number that is a multiple of all of the denominators in the equation.

Let's go back to the pizza example with a slight variation. We place an order for two pizzas and a new employee bakes our pizzas. He slices one pie in eighths (8/8) and one pie in sixths (6/6). If you eat two slices from each pie, how much pizza did you eat?

$$\frac{1}{8} + \frac{1}{8} + \frac{1}{6} + \frac{1}{6} = \frac{?}{?}$$

In this example, the common denominator must be a multiple of both 6 and 8. Each denominator in the equation is multiplied by a different number that results in the same product. This is a perfect time to review your multiplication tables, because we need to find which number is a multiple of both 6 and 8. We can determine that 6 and 8 are factors of 24. A *factor* is any of two or more numbers that can be multiplied together to get the product without a remainder—in this case, 24:

$$8 \times 3 = 24 \qquad 6 \times 4 = 24$$

The common denominator for 6 and 8 is thus 24. Now we adjust each number in our original equation to a fraction with the common denominator. This is done by multiplying each numerator and denominator by its respective *multiplier* to bring the denominator to 24. For $\frac{1}{8}$ we use the number 3.

$$\frac{1}{8} = \frac{3 \times 1}{3 \times 8} = \frac{3}{24}$$

One-eighth is equal to three twenty-fourths.

For $\frac{1}{6}$ we use the number 4.

$$\frac{1}{6} = \frac{4 \times 1}{4 \times 6} = \frac{4}{24}$$

One-sixth is equal to four twenty-fourths.

Now we can figure out how much pizza we ate. In our original equation, wherever we had $\frac{1}{8}$, we replace it with $\frac{3}{24}$. We replace $\frac{1}{6}$ with $\frac{4}{24}$. Then we add the numerators together.

$$\frac{3}{24} + \frac{3}{24} + \frac{4}{24} + \frac{4}{24} = \frac{14}{24}$$

Is there a number that we can divide into both 14 and 24 in order to reduce this fraction to its lowest terms? Yes, 2 is a factor of both 14 and 24.

$$\frac{14}{24} = \frac{14 / 2}{24 / 2} = \frac{7}{12}$$

Seven twelfths ($\frac{7}{12}$) is the total amount of pizza we ate by eating two slices from a pizza cut into eight slices and two slices from a pizza cut into six slices. Seven twelfths ($\frac{7}{12}$) is slightly more than one half.

**Subtraction with Fractions** Subtraction with fractions has the same rules as addition with fractions with respect to the issues of a common denominator and reducing a fraction to its lowest terms. All of the denominators in an equation must be the same before subtracting. For example, if you have three slices of a pizza that has been sliced into eight equal pieces, and a friend walks over and grabs one off your plate, you have just experienced subtraction:

$$\frac{3}{8} - \frac{1}{8} = \frac{2}{8}$$

We know that $\frac{2}{8}$ must be reduced to its lowest terms, so we divide the numerator and the denominator by 2.

$$\frac{2}{8} = \frac{2/2}{8/2} = \frac{1}{4}$$

After your friend swipes the third slice of pizza off your plate, you are left with two slices of pizza, or $\frac{1}{4}$ of the pizza.

If you happened to pick up one slice of pizza from the pizza that was cut into eight equal slices and two slices from the pizza that was cut into six equal slices, and your friend swipes a slice from the pizza cut into six slices, how much pizza is left on your plate?

$$\frac{1}{8} + \frac{2}{6} - \frac{1}{6} = \frac{?}{?}$$

The common denominator for eighths and sixths is 24. Next we convert all of our fractions to have the same common denominator.

$$\frac{1}{8} = \frac{1 \times 3}{8 \times 3} = \frac{3}{24} \qquad \frac{2}{6} = \frac{2 \times 4}{6 \times 4} = \frac{8}{24} \qquad \frac{1}{6} = \frac{1 \times 4}{6 \times 4} = \frac{4}{24}$$

Now that all of the fractions have the same common denominator, we can add and subtract our fractions.

$$\frac{3}{24} + \frac{8}{24} - \frac{4}{24} = \frac{7}{24}$$

The answer to this equation is $\frac{7}{24}$. Seven twenty-fourths cannot be reduced further because there is not a common factor that can be divided equally into both 7 and 24 except the number 1.

**Multiplication with Fractions** Multiplication is the easiest of all of the mathematical operations performed with fractions. The issue of a common denominator is of no concern with multiplication. First multiply all of the numerators in the equation, then multiply all of the denominators in the equation. Once this is complete, reduce the fraction to its lowest term.

We have just been called to cater a child's birthday party. The parent tells you that 24 children will be attending. She wants you to serve pizza. She asks you how many pizzas she needs to order to serve all of the children.

The average portion size of pizza for one child is two slices. Each pizza is cut into eight slices. For the children, we need:

$$\frac{2 \text{ (number of slices per child)}}{8 \text{ (number of slices in 1 pie)}} \times \frac{24 \text{ (number of children)}}{1} = \frac{48 \text{ (total number of slices)}}{8}$$

We need to reduce this improper fraction, $\frac{48}{8}$. This is accomplished by dividing 8 into 48.

$$48 \div 8 = 6$$

We need to order six pizza pies to feed 24 children two slices of pizza. In this case, the improper fraction is reduced to a whole number, not a mixed number.

**Division with Fractions** Division is a process different from any other mathematical operation with fractions. When dividing two fractions, the second fraction is inverted, and then the fractions are multiplied. Inverting the second fraction means switching the placement of the numerator with the denominator, and vice versa. The numerator becomes the denominator and the denominator becomes the numerator. Then multiply, following the rule for multiplication of fractions, and reduce the product to its lowest terms.

If we want to divide 1/3 by 1/4:

$$\frac{1}{3} \div \frac{1}{4} = \frac{1}{3} \times \frac{4}{1} = \frac{4}{3} = 1\tfrac{1}{3}$$

Four thirds, $\frac{4}{3}$, the solution to the division exercise above, is an improper fraction. It must be reduced to a mixed number. It is reduced by dividing the denominator into the numerator. One and one third, $1\frac{1}{3}$, is the mixed-number equivalent of 4/3.

## Mixed Numbers

A mixed number is a whole number with a fraction (a noninteger quantity). Basic mathematical operations for mixed numbers are the same as for fractions. However, when performing mathematical operations with mixed numbers, the mixed number must first be changed into an improper fraction.

Then, before adding or subtracting, all of the fractions must share a common denominator. Common denominators are not a concern with multiplication or division. When the mathematical operation is complete, the answer should be reduced to the lowest terms. If the answer is an improper fraction, it should be reduced to a mixed number.

**Addition with Mixed Numbers** Yesterday we roasted six prime rib roasts. One of the prime rib roasts was used to serve our dining room customers and five of the prime rib roasts were used to serve a banquet. There is one-quarter ($\frac{1}{4}$) of the prime rib roast left over from the dining room kitchen. There are one and one half ($1\frac{1}{2}$) prime rib roasts left over from the banquet kitchen. How much prime rib roast is left over from yesterday?

In order to determine how much prime rib roast is left over, we need to find a common denominator for the quantities $\frac{1}{2}$ and $\frac{1}{4}$ and the entire prime rib that is left over (1).

The common denominator is 4. All of the quantities need to be converted into fractions with the common denominator of 4. We multiply the number 1 by $\frac{4}{4}$, and the quantity $\frac{1}{2}$ by $\frac{2}{2}$. Then we add the fractions and reduce the sum to its lowest terms. Then we will know how much prime rib is left from yesterday.

$$\frac{1}{1} \times \frac{4}{4} = \frac{4}{4} \qquad \frac{1}{2} \times \frac{2}{2} = \frac{2}{4}$$

Then add:

$$\frac{4}{4} + \frac{2}{4} + \frac{1}{4} = \frac{7}{4}$$

The amount of prime rib roasts left over from yesterday is seven-fourths, ($\frac{7}{4}$). Seven-fourths ($\frac{7}{4}$) is an improper fraction because it represents a quantity where the numerator is greater than the denominator. Improper fractions should be reduced to a mixed number. In order to reduce an improper fraction to a mixed number, the denominator is divided into the numerator. In this example, 7 is divided by 4.

$$7 \div 4 = 1\tfrac{3}{4} \quad \text{or} \quad 4\overline{)7} = 1\tfrac{3}{4}$$

The mixed number is $1\frac{3}{4}$. There are $1\frac{3}{4}$ prime rib roasts left over from yesterday.

**Subtraction with Mixed Numbers** Common steam table pan sizes in a commercial kitchen are 200, 400, and 600. A 600 pan will hold three times as much as a 200 pan and 1½ times as much as a 400 pan. A recipe for macaroni and cheese yields enough product to fill a 600 pan. At the end of the day, the leftovers are transferred into 200 pans. If the leftover macaroni and cheese for today fill 1½ of a 200 pan, how much macaroni and cheese did we serve today?

A 600 pan equals three of a 200 pan, and we have 1½ 200 pans left over:

$$\frac{3\ (200\text{ pans})}{1} - 1\tfrac{1}{2}\ (200\text{ pans}) = \frac{3}{1} - \frac{3}{2}$$

$$= \frac{6}{2} - \frac{3}{2} = \frac{3}{2} = 1\tfrac{1}{2}\ 200\text{ pans}$$

We served 1½ 200 pans today, or half of a 600 pan.

**Multiplication with Mixed Numbers** We need to order new linen for our dining room. We can seat 150 patrons at one time. On a busy Saturday evening, we turn our tables 2½ times. We decide to order enough napkins to seat our dining room 3½ times. How many napkins do we need to order?

$$150\ (\text{seats}) \times 3\tfrac{1}{2} =$$

$$\frac{150}{1} \times \frac{7}{2} - \frac{1{,}050}{2} = 525\text{ napkins}$$

We need to order 525 napkins in order to have enough to seat our dining room 3½ times.

**Division with Mixed Numbers** We have 4½ trays of desserts and we need to divide the trays by ¼. How many times does ¼ divide into 4½?

$$4\tfrac{1}{2} \div \frac{1}{4} = \frac{9}{2} \times \frac{4}{1} = \frac{36}{2} = 18$$

One-quarter divided into 4½ exactly 18 times.

## BASIC MATHEMATICS 102: MIXED NUMBERS AND NONINTEGERS REVIEW PROBLEMS—FRACTIONS

Convert the following fractions to a decimal and a percentage.

1. $\frac{1}{2} =$

2. $\frac{1}{4} =$

3. $\frac{1}{3} =$

4. $\frac{1}{5} =$

5. $\frac{1}{10} =$

Add the following fractions with the same denominator.

6. $\frac{1}{4} + \frac{1}{4} =$

7. $\frac{1}{3} + \frac{2}{3} =$

8. $\frac{5}{8} + \frac{7}{8} =$

9. $\frac{5}{9} + \frac{8}{9} =$

Add the following fractions with different denominators.

10. $\frac{1}{4} + \frac{1}{3} =$

11. $\frac{1}{3} + \frac{7}{8} =$

12. $\frac{1}{4} + \frac{2}{3} =$

13. $\frac{1}{5} + \frac{2}{10} =$

Subtract the following fractions with the same denominator.

**14.** $\frac{2}{4} - \frac{1}{4} =$

**15.** $\frac{2}{3} - \frac{1}{3} =$

**16.** $\frac{7}{8} - \frac{5}{8} =$

**17.** $\frac{8}{9} - \frac{5}{9} =$

Subtract the following fractions with different denominators.

**18.** $\frac{1}{3} - \frac{1}{4} =$

**19.** $\frac{7}{8} - \frac{1}{3} =$

**20.** $\frac{2}{3} - \frac{1}{4} =$

**21.** $\frac{5}{10} - \frac{2}{20} =$

Multiply the following fractions.

**22.** $\frac{1}{4} \times \frac{1}{4} =$

**23.** $\frac{1}{3} \times \frac{2}{3} =$

**24.** $\frac{7}{8} \times \frac{1}{8} =$

**25.** $\frac{1}{2} \times \frac{1}{2} =$

Divide the following fractions.

**26.** $\frac{1}{4} \div \frac{1}{4} =$

**27.** $\frac{1}{3} \div \frac{2}{3} =$

**28.** $\frac{7}{8} \div \frac{1}{8} =$

**29.** $\frac{1}{2} \div \frac{1}{3} =$

## Basic Mathematics 102: Mixed Numbers and Nonintegers Review Answers—Fractions

**1.** $\frac{1}{2} = 1 \div 2 = .5 = 50\%$

Note that when converting .5 to 50%, you must add a zero before moving the decimal point two spaces to the right. This is the same as multiplying .5 by 100 ($.5 \times 100 = 50\%$).

**2.** $\frac{1}{4} = 1 \div 4 = .25 = 25\%$

**3.** $\frac{1}{3} = 1 \div 3 = .33 = 33\%$

**4.** $\frac{1}{5} = 1 \div 5 = .2 = 20\%$

**5.** $\frac{1}{10} = 1 \div 10 = .1 = 10\%$

**6.** $\frac{1}{4} + \frac{1}{4} = \frac{2}{4} = \frac{1}{2}$

**7.** $\frac{1}{3} + \frac{2}{3} = \frac{3}{3} = 1$

**8.** $\frac{5}{8} + \frac{7}{8} = \frac{12}{8} = 1\frac{4}{8} = 1\frac{1}{2}$

**9.** $\frac{5}{9} + \frac{8}{9} = \frac{13}{9} = 1\frac{4}{9}$

**10.** $\frac{1}{4} + \frac{1}{3} = \frac{3}{12} + \frac{4}{12} = \frac{7}{12}$

**11.** $\frac{1}{3} + \frac{7}{8} = \frac{8}{24} + \frac{21}{24} = \frac{29}{24} = 1\frac{5}{24}$

**12.** $\frac{1}{4} + \frac{2}{3} = \frac{3}{12} + \frac{8}{12} = \frac{11}{12}$

**13.** $\frac{1}{5} + \frac{2}{10} = \frac{2}{10} + \frac{2}{10} = \frac{4}{10} = \frac{2}{5}$

**14.** $\frac{2}{4} - \frac{1}{4} = \frac{1}{4}$

**15.** $\frac{2}{3} - \frac{1}{3} = \frac{1}{3}$

**16.** $\frac{7}{8} - \frac{5}{8} = \frac{2}{8} = \frac{1}{4}$

**17.** $\frac{8}{9} - \frac{5}{9} = \frac{3}{9} = \frac{1}{3}$

**18.** $\frac{1}{3} - \frac{1}{4} = \frac{4}{12} - \frac{3}{12} = \frac{1}{12}$

**19.** $\frac{7}{8} - \frac{1}{3} = \frac{21}{24} - \frac{8}{24} = \frac{13}{24}$

**20.** $\frac{2}{3} - \frac{1}{4} = \frac{8}{12} - \frac{3}{12} = \frac{5}{12}$

**21.** $\frac{5}{10} - \frac{2}{10} = \frac{10}{20} - \frac{2}{20} = \frac{8}{20} = \frac{2}{5}$

**22.** $\frac{1}{4} \times \frac{1}{4} = \frac{1}{16}$

**23.** $\frac{1}{3} \times \frac{2}{3} = \frac{2}{9}$

**24.** $\frac{7}{8} \times \frac{1}{8} = \frac{7}{64}$

**25.** $\frac{1}{2} \times \frac{1}{2} = \frac{1}{4}$

**26.** $\frac{1}{4} \div \frac{1}{4} = \frac{1}{4} \times \frac{4}{1} = \frac{4}{4} = 1$

**27.** $\frac{1}{3} \div \frac{2}{3} = \frac{1}{3} \times \frac{3}{2} = \frac{3}{6} = \frac{1}{2}$

**28.** $\frac{7}{8} \div \frac{1}{8} = \frac{7}{8} \times \frac{8}{1} = \frac{56}{8} = 7$

**29.** $\frac{1}{2} \div \frac{1}{3} = \frac{1}{2} \times \frac{3}{1} = \frac{3}{2} = 1\frac{1}{2}$

## Basic Mathematical Operations Using Decimals

A decimal is a number written with a decimal point. The decimal represents a number that is less than 1 (<1) or a mixed number that contains a whole number and a number that is less than 1. The key to performing mathematical operations with decimals is to be very careful with the placement of the decimal point.

Beverage inventory is an example of a time you would need to use decimals. A physical inventory of alcoholic-beverage bottles behind the bar is done monthly. The bottles are counted to accurately determine the cost of beverage sold each month. For each variety of product we sell, we count the number of full bottles and we either measure or estimate the amount of alcohol in bottles that are partially used.

**Addition with Decimals** Addition with decimals is very easy. The key is to line up the decimal points and then add. Let's continue with the beverage inventory example.

Our hotel has three beverage outlets. We are counting bottles of vodka. At the first bar, the only bottle is one-quarter full. There is .25 of a bottle of vodka. The second bar has 8 full bottles and a bottle that is half full. There are 8.5 bottles of vodka. The third bar has 10 full bottles and one-fifth of a bottle. There are 10.2 bottles of vodka (i.e., one-fifth, 1/5, is 2/10, or .2). How much vodka do we have in our three beverage outlets?

$$\begin{array}{r} 0.25 \\ +\ 8.50 \\ \underline{10.20} \\ 18.95 \end{array}$$

We have 18.95 bottles of vodka in our three beverage outlets. (Zeros can be used to help to keep the decimal points in the correct column.)

**Subtraction with Decimals** Subtraction with decimals is as easy as addition, and the same rule applies. Line up the decimal points and subtract.

Several customers are served while we are at the second bar counting the inventory. Before we leave, we double-check the vodka bottles. We notice that the partially filled bottle is empty and one of the full bottles is three-quarters full, or .75. The partial bottle was .50 full and the new partial bottle is .25 empty. We need to subtract .75 from our prior total.

$$\begin{array}{r} 18.95 \\ \underline{-00.75} \\ 18.20 \end{array}$$

Our inventory of vodka in our three beverage outlets is now 18.2 bottles.

**Multiplication with Decimals** Multiplication with decimals is the same as multiplication with whole numbers, with one exception.

Once the multiplication is complete, the number of decimal places in the equation are counted. Then a decimal point is inserted equal to the total number of decimal places in the equation.

We have 18.2 bottles of vodka in our beverage outlets. We paid \$4.65 per bottle. What is the total cost of the vodka inventory?

$$\begin{array}{rl} \$4.65 & \text{(2 decimal places)} \\ \underline{\times 18.2} & \text{(1 decimal place)} \\ \$84.630 & \text{(3 decimal places)} \end{array}$$

There are two decimal places in \$4.65 and one decimal places in 18.2. Therefore, the answer needs to have three decimal places. The product of this equation is 84.630. When we write down the total cost of vodka inventory, we drop the final zero because we only use two decimal places with money. The cost is \$84.63.

**Division with Decimals** Division with decimals is the same as division with any whole numbers, with one exception. Before the problem is calculated, the decimal point needs to be inserted. There are 16.25 cases of vodka in beverage storage. The total value of vodka in inventory is \$906.75. How much does one case cost?

$$16.25\ \overline{)906.75}$$

This is the format for long division. In this format, we move the decimal point to the right equally on each side of the division sign. Each side of the equation has two decimal places, so we move the final decimal place over by two places. The equation now looks like this:

$$1625\ \overline{)90675}$$

As the problem is completed, the decimal point is inserted when the answer contains a quantity less than 1 (<1).

\$906.75 (dollar value of vodka)/16.25 (number of cases in inventory) = \$55.80 (case price)

## Basic Mathematical Operations Using Percentages

A percentage is a portion or a part of the whole. A percentage, in mathematical terms, is a fraction or ratio, with 100 understood to be the denominator.

$$1\% = .01 \qquad 1\% = \frac{1}{100}$$

Percentages are commonly used in food service because the majority of food products that we serve to our guests are a percentage of the original item we purchased. Percentages are easiest to use if they are converted to a decimal.

The conversion of a percentage to a decimal is easy. The general rule is to divide the number by 100.

$$87\% = \frac{87}{100} \qquad \frac{87}{100} = .87$$

The easiest way to do this is to remove the percent sign and move the decimal point right two places.

$$87\% = .87$$

In food service, the most common mathematical use of percentages is multiplying and dividing.

**Multiplication with Percentages** Multiplication with percentages is a simple process. The key is to remember that, most often, a percentage represents a number less than 1 ($<1$). When we multiply by a number less than 1, the answer is going to be a number smaller than the original number in the equation.

For example, a recipe serves 100 guests. The recipe calls for 2 gallons of tomato sauce. We have a banquet for 50 guests. We need to use 50 percent of the quantity of ingredients to serve 100. How many gallons of tomato sauce do we need to serve 50 guests?

2 (number of gallons to serve 100) $\times$ 50%
= 1 (number of gallons to serve 50)

*or*

We can convert the percentage to a decimal, 50% = .50, and multiply by .50.

2 (number of gallons to serve 100) $\times$ .50
= 1 (number of gallons to serve 50)

A percentage can represent a number equal to 1 ($=1$). One hundred percent is equal to 1. We can multiply by 100%, but there really is no point in multiplying by the number 1.

$$100\% = \frac{100}{100} = \frac{1}{1} = 1 \qquad 100\% = 1.00 = 1$$

A percentage can represent a number greater than 1 ($>1$). If we multiply by a number greater than 1, the answer will be greater than the original numbers in the equation.

Some food products expand as they cook. The amount of product available to serve to the guest is greater after cooking. An example of this is rice. Instant white rice has a yield percentage of 420 percent. This percentage represents a number greater than 1. When you convert 420 percent to a decimal, it becomes

$$\frac{420}{100} = 4.20 \qquad \textit{or} \qquad 420\% = 4.20$$

A recipe for a rice dish serves 32 guests. It calls for 2 pounds of uncooked rice. The yield on rice is 420 percent. How many pounds of cooked rice will 2 pounds of uncooked rice yield?

2 (pounds of uncooked rice) × 420% = 8.4 (pounds of cooked rice)

2 (pounds of uncooked rice) × 4.20 = 8.4 (pounds of cooked rice)

**Division with Percentages** Division with percentages is also a simple process. The percentage, or its equivalent decimal, is the divisor. If the percentage is less than 1 ($<1$), the answer will be greater than the dividend in the original equation.

We purchase a meat item for $1.69 a pound. The product has a 72-percent yield. This means that only 72 percent of the product is available to serve to the guest after the product is cooked. How much does it actually cost us, per pound, to serve this product to our guests?

$1.69 (price per pound) / 72% = $2.35

*or*

$1.69 (price per pound) / .72 = $2.35

In order to have one pound of this product to serve to our guests, we need to spend $2.35. If the percentage, or its equivalent decimal, is greater than 1 ($>1$), the answer will be smaller than the original dividend.

The instant white rice that we cooked earlier has a yield of 420 percent. We purchase rice for $1.00 a pound. How much does it cost us, per pound, to serve rice to our guests?

$1.00 (price per pound) / 420% = $0.24

*or*

$1.00 (price per pound) / 4.20 = $0.24

It costs $0.24 per pound to serve the guest rice after it is cooked.

## BASIC MATHEMATICS 102: MIXED NUMBERS AND NONINTEGERS REVIEW PROBLEMS—DECIMALS AND PERCENTAGES

Add the following:

| | | | |
|---|---|---|---|
| 1. .25 | 2. 1.33 | 3. .95 | 4. 2.42 |
| .65 | 2.46 | 1.89 | 1.36 |
| +.95 | + .50 | + .97 | + .97 |

Subtract the following:

| | | | |
|---|---|---|---|
| 5. 1.25 | 6. 2.40 | 7 6.50 | 8. 7.89 |
| − .75 | −1.89 | −3.39 | −4.32 |

Multiply the following using the decimal and then using the percent:

| | | | |
|---|---|---|---|
| 9. 1.39 | 10. 2.89 | 11. 3.59 | 12. 2.59 |
| × .67 (67%) | × .80 (80%) | × .40 (40%) | × .62 (62%) |

Divide the following using the decimal and then using the percent:

| | | | |
|---|---|---|---|
| 13. 1.39 / .67 (67%) | 14. 2.89 / .80 (80%) | 15. 3.59 / .40 (40%) | 16. 2.59 / .62 (62%) |

### Basic Mathematics 102: Mixed Numbers and Nonintegers Review Answers—Decimals and Percentages

**1.** 1.85
**2.** 4.29
**3.** 3.51
**4.** 4.75
**5.** 0.50
**6.** 0.51
**7.** 3.11
**8.** 3.57
**9.** 0.9313, 0.9313
**10.** 2.3120, 2.3120
**11.** 1.4360, 1.4360
**12.** 1.6058, 1.6058
**13.** 2.0746, 2.0746
**14.** 3.6125, 3.6125
**15.** 8.9750, 8.9750
**16.** 4.1774, 4.1774

# BASIC MATHEMATICS 103: FOOD-SERVICE-SPECIFIC MATHEMATICAL TERMINOLOGY

Culinarians need to understand certain mathematical terms and symbols. Some of the terms explain what type of information we will receive after performing the correct mathematical calculation. Some of these symbols express the relationship between two numbers.

## Product Yield

*Product yield* means that, on average, every time we purchase a certain food product and process or cook it the same way, we will have the same amount of product to serve to our guests.

A local bakery is famous for its apple pies. The pies are made with Granny Smith apples and are baked in a 9-inch shell. Granny Smith apples are purchased by the 40-pound case. One apple pie needs 2.5 pounds of apples. How many apples pies can we make from a case of apples?

40 (pounds per case) / 2.5 (pounds per pie)
= 16 (number of pies a case of apples yields)

Each time, on average, the bakery buys a case of Granny Smith apples to bake pies, 16 pies can be made. The product yield from one case of Granny Smith apples is 16 pies.

Each Thanksgiving the bakery sells 300 apple pies. How many cases of Granny Smith apples need to be purchased in order to produce 300 apple pies?

300 (number of pies needed) / 16 (number of pies per case)
= 18.75 cases*

*18.75 needs to be rounded up to a whole case.

The bakery needs to purchase 19 cases of Granny Smith apples in order to have enough apples to bake 300 pies.

The "Best in the West" Coffee Shop serves an 8-ounce portion of pork tenderloin. The pork tenderloin is purchased oven-ready with an average weight of 8 pounds. After the tenderloin is baked, on average, it weighs 7 pounds. How many 8-ounce portions can we serve from each tenderloin?

7 (pounds, cooked) × 16 (ounces in one pound)
= 112 (ounces in 7 pounds)

112 (total ounces) / 8 (portion size)
= 14 (number of portions that can be served)

Each time, on average, we purchase an 8-pound pork tenderloin, we can serve 14 portions. The product yield from one tenderloin is 14 portions.

The chef at the "Best in the West" is preparing for a busy holiday weekend. In the last holiday weekend, 196 orders of pork tenderloin were sold. If we plan to sell 196 orders this weekend, how many pork tenderloins do we need to purchase?

196 (anticipated number of portions)
/ 14 (number of portions per tenderloin) = 14 (tenderloins needed)

## Recipe Yield and Recipe Conversions

The term *recipe yield* refers to the total weight, volume, count, or number of portions a properly prepared recipe should serve. Recipe yield is critically important in production planning. It is impossible for a chef to plan how much food to purchase and to prepare if there is no knowledge of how much a recipe will produce.

The pork tenderloin produces 7 pounds of cooked tenderloin and yields 14 portions, each of which is 8 ounces. This is an example of a recipe that yields a certain weight and number of portions.

A soup recipe yields 2 gallons. This recipe has a volume yield. If we serve an 8-ounce bowl of soup, how many portions can we serve?

2 (gallons) × 128 (ounces in 1 gallon) = 256 (ounces in 2 gallons)

256 (ounces in 2 gallons) / 8 (ounces in 1 portion)
= 32 (total portions)

The soup recipe yields thirty-two 8-ounce portions.

For the apple pies we read about earlier, each case of apples produced 16 pies. This is an example of a recipe that yields a certain count. If your restaurant purchases these pies and slices them in eight pieces, each pie can serve eight guests.

It is not uncommon to need to adjust the yield on a recipe to produce more or less portions. Any time we need to adjust the yield on a recipe, we need to adjust the quantity of ingredients we use in the recipe. This is a simple process:

$$\frac{\text{New yield}}{\text{Old yield}} = \text{Multiplier}$$

The *multiplier* is the number that we multiply our ingredients by to adjust the yield of the recipe. A recipe for potato salad yields 50 portions. We have been asked to cater a picnic for 125 people. We want to serve the potato salad. What quantity of ingredients should we use?

$$\frac{125 \text{ (new yield)}}{50 \text{ (old yield)}} = 2.5 \text{ (multiplier)}$$

The multiplier, 2.5, tells us that we need 2 1/2 times the ingredient quantity in the recipe to serve 50 in order to have the recipe serve 125. If the recipe that yields 50 portions uses 20 pounds of potatoes, how many pounds of potatoes do we need to yield 125 portions?

$$20 \text{ (pounds for 50)} \times 2.5 \text{ (multiplier)} = 50 \text{ (pounds of potatoes to serve 125)}$$

We need 50 pounds of potatoes to serve 125 portions of potato salad.

Using the multiplier to increase or decrease the quantity of ingredients is necessary for all products. However, herbs, spices, and seasonings can present a problem when recipes are adjusted by a great quantity. These should be adjusted with caution.

## Rounding

When we perform a mathematical operation on a group of numbers, the answer is not always going to be a whole number. The chances are, we will round the answer up or down. The general rule for rounding in mathematics is based on the number 5. If the answer to a problem is a whole number plus a decimal equal to or greater than .5, (= or > .5), we round up. If the answer to a problem is a whole number and a decimal less than .5, (<.5), we round down. This rule applies to mathematics and is a good rule to follow under most circumstances. The plate cost for an entree item adds up to $2.256. Rounding up, the plate cost is now $2.26. The plate cost for an entree item adds up to $2.254. Rounding down, the plate cost is now $2.25.

In food service, however, when you are figuring out how much food to purchase or how much food to prepare, I urge you to use caution when you are rounding. The exact mathematical answer does not take into account the fact that a server might drop a plate, or a cook might burn a sauce. When you are rounding in food service, rounding up is probably the better option.

## Conversions using Multipliers

The understanding and use of a multiplier in a food service operation can assist with recipe conversations and product costing. Let's explore the relationship between a liter and a quart. A liter contains 33.8 ounces, while a quart contains 32 ounces. A liter is 1.8 ounces greater than a quart, but what is the mathematical relationship?

33.8 (ounces in a liter) / 32 (ounces in a quart) = 1.056

1 liter = 1.056 quarts

One liter is 1.056 of one quart. This makes it easy to convert from quarts to liters. In the United States, we buy gasoline by the gallon. There are 4 quarts in gallon. In Europe, gasoline is purchased by the liter. If we want to compare the cost of gasoline between the United States and Europe, we can use the multiplier 1.056.

A gallon of gas at a U.S. gas station costs $1.459. One quart costs

$1.459 (cost per gallon) / 4 (quarts per gallon) = .3648 per quart

The equivalent cost for a liter of gas at a European gas station would be 1.056 times a U.S. quart price.

$0.3648 (cost per quart) × 1.056 (multiplier for quart to liter)
= $0.3852 equivalent liter price

The relationship of a quart to a liter is

32 (ounces per quart) / 33.8 (ounces per liter) = .9467

1 quart = .9467 liters

If the U.S. dollar price for gasoline in Europe is $3.50 per liter, what would our gas pump price have to be to equal Europe's gas prices?

$3.50 (price per liter in Europe)
× .9467 (multiplier for liter to quart) = $3.3135 per quart

multiplied by 4, because there are 4 quarts in one gallon:

$3.3135 (cost per quart) × 4 (number of quarts per gallon)
= $13.25 cost for a gallon of gasoline based on the European cost per liter

A multiplier can be developed for any two numbers that have a constant relationship. The example of liter to quart or quart to liter is based on a unit of measure that never changes. A multiplier can be developed to express the relationship of edible and as-served food product based on the as-purchased amount of food. This will be explored further in Chapter 4.

Once the multiplier is developed, whenever you want to convert units of measure or price, all you need to do is multiply.

## Greater Than, Less Than

Throughout the chapter, we have occasionally used the symbols $>1$ or $<1$ to indicate that a ratio is greater than or less than 1. We can also use those symbols to indicate that some numbers are larger or smaller than others. The number 20 is greater than the number 10, $20 > 10$. The number 10 is smaller or less than 20, $10 < 20$.

The relationship of one number or numbers to another is important to understand. If we know that a mathematical calculation should give us a number that is greater than ($>$) or less than ($<$) the numbers in the problem, we can begin to determine if we made a mistake in our calculations. The following sections provide the rules for checking our math using the greater-than or less-than functions. These rules hold true in culinary mathematics because we always deal in positive numbers (you cannot have negative carrots); in other fields of mathematics, the rules would not be as clear-cut.

**Addition** If we add two numbers together, the sum must be greater than ($>$) the numbers we are adding.

$$20 + 10 = x, \quad x \text{ equals a number} > 20, \quad x = 30$$

If the sum we arrive at is not greater than 20, we know we have made a mistake.

**Subtraction** If we subtract one number from another, the difference must be less than ($<$) the largest number in the equation.

$$20 - 10 = x, \quad x \text{ equals a number} < 20, \quad x = 10$$

If the answer is not less than 20, we know we have made a mistake.

## Multiplication

Multiplication for food service has a few simple rules. If we multiply any number by a number that is greater than the number 1 ($>1$) the answer will be greater than the numbers in the problem.

$$10 \times 2 = x, \quad x \text{ equals a number} > 2 \text{ or } 10, \quad x = 20$$

If we multiply any number by a number that is less than 1 (<1), a fraction, a decimal or a percentage, then the equation will result in a number that is smaller or less than (<) the original number.

$20 \times (1/2, \text{ or } .50 \text{ or } 50\%) = x, \quad x$ equals a number $< 20, \quad x = 10$

$$\frac{20}{1} \times \frac{1}{2} = \frac{20}{2} = \frac{10}{1}$$

$$20 \times .50 = 10$$

$$20 \times 50\% = 10$$

**Division** Division yields similar results to multiplication, but in reverse. If you divide the numerator by a denominator greater than 1 (>1) the answer will be smaller or less than (<) the original numerator.

$20/2 = x, \quad x$ equals a number $< 20, \quad x = 10$

If we divide the numerator by a denominator that is less than 1 (<1), a fraction, a decimal, or a percentage, the equation will result in a number that is greater than (>) the original numerator.

$10/(1/2, \text{ or } .50 \text{ or } 50\%) = x, \quad x$ equals a number $> 10, \quad x = 20$

$$\frac{10}{1} / \frac{1}{2} = \frac{20}{1}$$

$$10 / .50 = 20$$

$$10 / 50\% = 20$$

If we truly have an understanding that a mathematical problem should yield a number that is greater than (>) or less than (<) the original numbers in a problem, then we can determine if we chose the correct mathematical operation. If the answer is incorrect, chances are that we multiplied instead of divided or divided instead of multiplied.

A thorough understanding of basic mathematics can make you a successful food service operator.

## BASIC MATHEMATICS 103: FOOD-SERVICE-SPECIFIC MATHEMATICAL TERMINOLOGY REVIEW PROBLEMS

### Product Yield

A recipe for cranberry relish contains one 5-pound bag of cranberries and other ingredients. If the recipe is prepared correctly, it produces 7 pounds of cranberry relish. On average, 56 guests can each be served one-eighth (1/8) of a pound of cranberry relish from the one 5-pound bag of cranberries and other ingredients in this recipe.

Next week is Thanksgiving, and we have reservations for 350 guests who are going to be served, among other things, one-eighth (1/8) of a pound of cranberry relish. How many 5-pound bags of cranberries do we need to order so that all of our guests can be served?

Should we consider rounding the number of bags of cranberries up? Or down? Why?

### Recipe Yield and Recipe Conversions

A recipe for Texas chili yields 3 gallons. We serve a 6-ounce portion of Texas chili in a bread bowl. How many portions can we serve from each completed recipe?

We have been asked to cater a tailgate party for the local high-school championship football game. Attendance at the championship game last year was 500. The menu is Texas chili. Using the information from the recipe yield above, what multiplier do we need to use in order to produce enough Texas chili to serve 500 football fans?

Should we consider rounding the multiplier up? Or down? Why?

### Developing a Multiplier

A multiplier expresses the relationship between two quantities that do not change. As covered in the text, the relationship between a liter and a quart is a constant. It will not change. The relationship between a gallon and a quart is a constant. It will not change. What is the relationship of a gallon to a quart, and what number (multiplier) expresses that relationship?

The relationship of a quart to a gallon is a constant. It will not change. What is the relationship of a quart to a gallon, and what quantity (multiplier) expresses this relationship?

## Basic Mathematics 103: Food-Service-Specific Mathematical Terminology Review Answers

### Product Yield

A 5-pound bag of cranberries produces enough to serve 56 guests. To serve 350 guests, how many 5-pound bags of cranberries do we need?

350 (portions to serve) / 56 (portions per 5-pound bag) = 6.25 bags of cranberries

Six and one quarter (6.25) 5-pound bags of cranberries will make enough cranberry relish to serve 350 guests.

Should we round down to six bags? Should we round up to seven bags? Why?

It would be wise to round up to seven bags. Cranberries are not an expensive food product. The extra cost is about $1.00 per pound, or an additional $5.00. Chances are, a certain number of guests will ask for more cranberry relish. It is also likely that we will feed our staff a holiday dinner. It is much better for customer relations to have more food than we need than to run out of an item the guest wants.

### Recipe Yield and Recipe Conversion

If a recipe produces 3 gallons of chili, how many 6-ounce portions can it serve?

3 (gallons) × 128 (ounces per gallon) = 384 ounces in 3 gallons

384 (ounces in 3 gallons) / 6 (ounces per portion) = 64 portions

Sixty-four 6-ounce portions of Texas chili can be served from a recipe that yields 3 gallons of chili.

If we cater a party for 500 and we serve 6-ounce portions of Texas chili, what number do we need to multiply all of the ingredients in the recipe by to yield 500 portions?

$$\frac{500 \text{ (new yield)}}{64 \text{ (old yield)}} = 7.8125 \text{ (multiplier)}$$

If we multiply all of the ingredients by 7.8125, the recipe will yield 50 portions.

Should we round the multiplier up to 8? Why? The multiplier should be rounded to 8. It is much easier to multiply by the number 8 than by the number 7.8125. If we round up to 8, the recipe will yield 512 portions. This will cover a few spills, as well as feeding the staff.

### Developing a Multiplier

What is the relationship of a gallon to a quart? One gallon has 128 ounces and one quart has 32 ounces.

128 (ounces) / 32 (ounces) = 4

One (1) gallon equals four (4) quarts. Any time you are converting from a quart to a gallon, the multiplier is the number 4. If a recipe yields a quart of sauce and you need the recipe to yield a gallon of sauce, you can multiply all of the ingredients by the number 4.

What is the relationship between a quart and a gallon? One quart is 32 ounces and one gallon is 128 ounces.

32 (ounces) / 128 (ounces) = .25 (25%, 1/4)

One (1) quart is .25, 25 percent, or 1/4 of a gallon. Anytime you are converting from a gallon to a quart, the multiplier is .25, 25 percent, or 1/4.

If a recipe yields a gallon of stock and you need one quart, you can multiply all of the ingredients by .25, 25 percent, or 1/4.

# Chapter 2
# UNITS OF MEASURE

Repeat customers are the key to success in a food service operation. Customers return because they enjoy the food and service and perceive they receive value for the menu price. Repeat customers generally know the static menu offerings and quite often have a favorite dish. Some repeat customers order the same menu item each time they visit the restaurant. The repeat customer expects the static menu items to be consistent. Consistency means the taste, texture, portion size, and overall look and feel of the item is exactly the same each time they visit.

The best way to ensure a consistent product is to use a standardized recipe. One key to successfully using standardized recipes is to accurately measure all of the ingredients in the recipe and the portion size before it is plated. Accuracy of measurement is critical to portion control, portion costing, and menu pricing.

The proper way to accurately measure a liquid is to use a volume unit of measure. The proper way to accurately measure a solid item is to use a scale. This issue can be complicated for two reasons. The first reason has to do with the actual units of measure used. The tradition in the United States has been to use a different system for units of measure than the international community.

The second reason is that all written recipes do not correctly measure ingredients. It is not uncommon for a recipe to list a solid ingredient with a volume unit of measure. The most common example of this is a cup of flour. A cup is a volume unit of measure. Flour should be weighed.

## U.S. STANDARD UNITS OF MEASURE

**FIGURE 2.1** U.S. volume units of measure (clockwise from top): one gallon, one-half gallon, one quart, one pint. Photography by Thomas Myers.

### Volume Units of Measure

Liquids are measured by volume. Liquids include products such as water, juice, oil, and stock. The traditional volume units of measure in the United States are gallon, quart, pint, cup, fluid ounce, tablespoon, and teaspoon. The relationship between these volume units of measure is shown in Table 2.1.

When measuring liquids for food preparation, volume containers are filled to the desired level. The basic measuring tools are units from 1 gallon to 1 cup along with tablespoons and teaspoons.

When we portion foods for service that are "liquid" in nature—like soup, chili, or stew—the service ware that we use controls the portion size. A bowl or cup can only hold so many fluid ounces; therefore, the portion size is controlled by the size of the bowl or cup.

A sauce that is placed over an entree or a vegetable is also a liquid measure and is controlled by a volume unit of measure. The tool that we use to measure a portion of a sauce is a ladle. Ladles come in a variety of sizes, from ½ fluid ounce to 32 fluid ounces. The common ladle sizes used to portion are ½ fl. oz., 1 fl. oz., 2 fl. oz., 3 fl. oz., 6 fl. oz., and 8 fl. oz. Larger-size ladles are generally used in the cooking process and not as a portion-control tool.

**TABLE 2.1**

U.S. Volume Units of Measure and Their Equivalents

| *Gallon (G, gal)* | *Quart (qt)* | *Pint (pt)* | *Cup (C, c)* | *Fluid Ounce (fl. oz.)* | *Tablespoon (T, tbsp)* | *Teaspoon (t, tsp)* |
|---|---|---|---|---|---|---|
| 1 gallon | 4 quarts | 8 pints | 16 cups | 128 fl. oz. | | |
| 1/2 gallon | 2 quarts | 4 pints | 8 cups | 64 fl. oz. | | |
| | 1 quart | 2 pints | 4 cups | 32 fl. oz. | | |
| | | 1 pint | 2 cups | 16 fl. oz. | | |
| | | | 1 cup | 8 fl. oz. | 16 T | |
| | | | 1/2 cup | 4 fl. oz. | 8 T | |
| | | | 1/4 cup | 2 fl. oz. | 4 T | |
| | | | | 1 fl. oz. | 2 T | |
| | | | | | 1 T | 3 tsp. |

A disher/scoop is another volume unit of measure commonly used as a portion-control tool. Dishers/scoops come in a variety of sizes, from a number 60, which is ½ fl. oz., to a number 6, which is ⅔ cup. The disher/scoop size is based on how many scoops you can serve from 1 quart. The interesting thing about dishers/scoops and portion control is that, other than ice cream, they are often used for products that are solid in nature. The best example I can give you is a serving of mashed potatoes that is scooped onto a plate, then pressed down and covered with gravy that is portioned from a ladle.

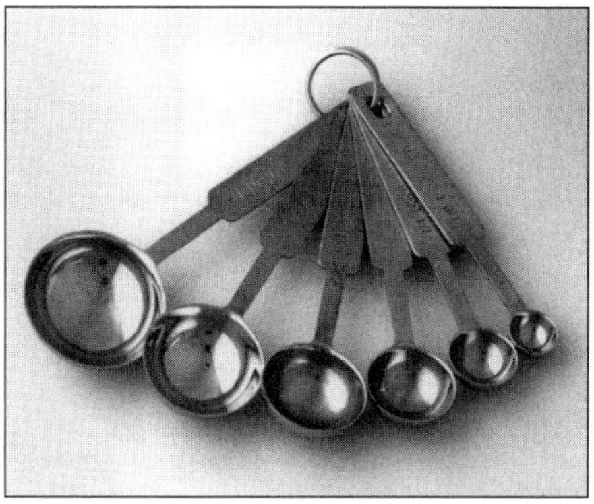

**FIGURE 2.2** U.S. volume units of measure (from left to right): tablespoon, teaspoon, and partial units of a teaspoon.
Photography by Thomas Myers.

## Weight Units of Measure

Solids are measured by weight. Solids include items such as meat, produce, flour, and sugar. The traditional units of measure for weight in the United States are pounds and ounces. With respect to weight, the word *ounce* refers to a portion or percentage of a pound. (A weight ounce is not the equivalent of a volume fluid ounce.) The relationship of these weight units of measure is shown in Table 2.2.

The only way to accurately weigh an item is to use a scale. Therefore, when measuring solids, we always use a scale. Accurate weight measurements is most critical in baking because of the chemical reactions that take place when the ingredients are placed in the oven.

Spices are a common group of solid item that are measured using volume units of measure. Some quantities of spices used in a recipe are so small that it becomes difficult to accurately weigh them. Therefore, we use a tablespoon, teaspoon, or a portion a teaspoon as the unit of measure.

**FIGURE 2.3** Bowls, a cup, and a crock.
Photography by Thomas Myers.

**FIGURE 2.4** Nested ladles: 32 ounces to 1 ounce.
Photography by Thomas Myers.

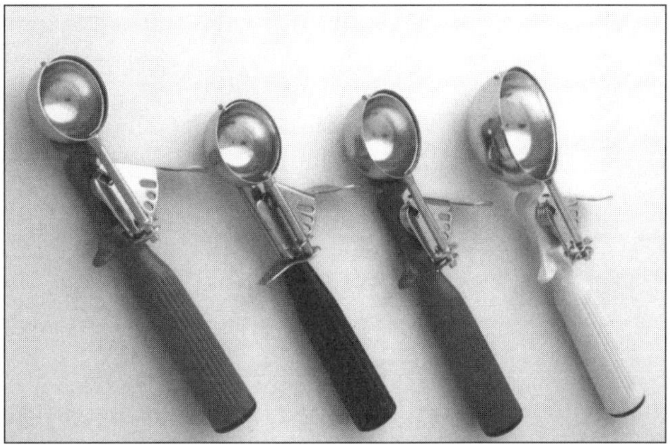

**FIGURE 2.5** Dishers/scoops: Sizes (from left to right) 10, 24, 30, and 40.
Photography by Thomas Myers.

**TABLE 2.2**

U.S. Weight Units of Measure and Their Equivalents

| *Pounds (lb. #)* | *Ounces (oz.)* |
|---|---|
| 1 pound | 16 ounces |
| 1/2 pound | 8 ounces |
| 1/4 pound | 4 ounces |
| 1/8 pound | 2 ounces |

**FIGURE 2.6** Baker's scale. Courtesy the Edlund Co. Photography by Thomas Myers.

**FIGURE 2.7** Portioning scale. Courtesy the Edlund Co.
Photography by Thomas Myers.

The portioning of food items like shaved turkey breast or ham for a sandwich is measured using a portioning scale.

### Count as a Unit of Measure

Certain types of food products are "measured" by count. These products lend themselves to counting because they are individual units. Eggs, shrimp, fruit, and bay leaves are examples of items that we commonly count. Counting is not a precise unit of measure, as volume or weight measurement are. In recipes where accuracy is critical, the amount of eggs may be measured by volume or even weight. Fruit, too, can be measured in a volume unit or weighed on a scale.

## INTERNATIONAL STANDARD UNITS OF MEASURE: THE METRIC SYSTEM

The *metric system* is the standard internationally recognized system for measurement. The metric system is a decimal-based system where the relationship between the units of measure are based on the number 10. The U.S. monetary system is a decimal-based system, but our traditional units of measure are not. Globalization of trade is encouraging U.S.-based businesses to switch to internationally recognized units of measure.

## Volume Units of Measure

In the metric system, the standard volume units of measure are the liter and milliliter. These volume units of measure are used worldwide, except in the United States. Alcoholic beverages are packaged exclusively using metric volume units of measure. The U.S. beverage industry purchases alcoholic beverages by the liter, 750 milliliter, or 500 milliliter size, but measures and sells mixed drinks by the fluid ounce.

If you look on the label of any liquid item, it is common to see both the traditional United States and the internationally recognized volume unit of measure listed. If you purchase an imported "liquid" item, such as olive oil from Italy, it is possible that the unit of measure will be in liters and not quarts or gallons. Table 2.3 lists the metric volume units of measure with the traditional U.S. equivalent.

The conversion from liter/milliliter to gallon/quart/fluid ounce is an approximation due to rounding. Understanding the similarities between the two different volume measuring systems is what is important. One liter is close to 1 quart, and 30 milliliters is approximately 1 fluid ounce.

In U.S. kitchens, it is common to find both U.S. standard and metric system quantities marked on our volume-measuring devices for cooking or portioning.

**TABLE 2.3**

Metric Volume Units of Measure and U.S. Equivalents

| *Liter (L)* | *Milliliter (mL)* | *Fluid Ounce* | *Gallon* | *Quart* | *Pint* | *Cup* | *Tablespoon* | *Teaspoon* |
|---|---|---|---|---|---|---|---|---|
| 3.8 L | 3800 mL | 128 fl. oz. | 1 gallon | | | | | |
| 1 L | 1000 mL | 33.8 fl. oz. | | | | | | |
| .95 L | 946 mL | 32 fl. oz. | | 1 quart | | | | |
| | 750 mL | 25.4 fl. oz. | | | | | | |
| | 500 mL | 16.9 fl. oz. | | | | | | |
| .47 L | 474 mL | 16 fl. oz. | | | 1pint | | | |
| .24 L | 237 mL | 8 fl. oz. | | | | 1 cup | | |
| | 30 mL | 1 fl. oz. | | | | | | |
| | 15 mL | | | | | | 1 T | |
| | 5 mL | | | | | | | 1 tsp. |

**TABLE 2.4**

Metric Weight Units of Measure and U.S. Equivalents

| *Kilogram (kg)* | *Gram (g)* | *Pound (lb, #)* | *Ounce (oz)* |
|---|---|---|---|
| 1 kilogram | 1000 grams | 2.2 pounds | 35.2 ounces |
| | 454 grams | 1 pound | 16 ounces |
| | 28.35 grams | | 1 ounce |
| | 1 gram | | .035 ounce |

### Weight Units of Measure

The metric system units of measure for weight are the kilogram and gram. If you look on the label of any item sold by weight, it is common to see both the traditional United States and the internationally recognized units of measure for weight listed. If you purchase an imported item, such as truffles from France, it is possible that the only unit of measure on the label will be in grams and not pounds or ounces. Table 2.4 lists the international units of measure for weight and the traditional U.S. equivalents.

If a recipe is written using metric weight units of measure, a scale that weighs in kilograms and grams should be used or the recipe should be converted to the U.S. standard units of measure.

## CONVERSION BETWEEN TRADITIONAL UNITED STATES UNITS OF MEASURE AND THE METRIC SYSTEM

**TABLE 2.5**

U.S./Metric Conversion Multipliers

| *Multiply* | *By* | *To Find* |
|---|---|---|
| **Volume Units** | | |
| Gallons | 3.7853 | Liters |
| Liters | 1.0567 | Quarts |
| Quarts | .946 | Liters |
| Pints | .474 | Liters |
| Cups | .237 | Liters |
| **Weight Units** | | |
| Kilograms | 2.2046 | Pounds |
| Pounds | .4536 | Kilograms |
| Grams | .0022 | Pounds |
| Pounds | 453.5924 | Grams |
| Grams | .0353 | Ounces |
| Ounces | 28.3495 | Grams |

The United States is definitely a part of the international community. As such, we are slowly leaning toward adopting the metric, or at least coexisting system in the metric world. In culinary publications, it is common to see recipes whose ingredients are listed in both the traditional U.S. quantities and their metric equivalent. The relationships between the units of measure are constant, so a multiplier can be developed to express these relationships. The easiest way to convert a recipe from the traditional U.S. units of measure to the metric system units of measure, or vice versa, is to use a multiplier, provided in Table 2.5.

The conversion process becomes a basic multiplication problem with decimals. A traditional U.S. unit of measure is converted into a metric unit of measure, or vice versa. These conversion decimals can be used to adjust unit prices from traditional U.S. unit pricing to metric unit pricing, and vice versa.

A recipe for cream of broccoli soup yields 2 gallons. How many liters are there in 2 gallons? Use the multiplier that converts gallons to liters.

2 (gallons) × 3.7853 (multiplier) = 7.57 liters

The cream of broccoli soup yields 7.75 liters.

A recipe for rye bread lists the quantity of rye flour as 500 grams. You do not have a scale that measures grams. You need to find out how many pounds and/or ounces there are in 500 grams. Use the multiplier that converts grams to ounces.

500 (grams) × .0353 (multiplier) = 17.65 ounces

The ounce equivalent of 500 grams is 17.65. There are 16 ounces in 1 pound. We need 1 pound, 1.65 ounces of rye flour for this recipe.

We purchased 2 liters of imported olive oil for $4.50. Our salad-dressing recipe uses 1 pint of olive oil. How much does it cost for 1 pint of olive oil? Use the multiplier that converts pints to liters.

$4.50 (cost for 2 liters) / 2 (liters) = $2.25 per liter

One liter of imported olive oil costs $2.25. How much is 1 pint?

$2.25 (cost for 1 liter) × .474 (multiplier)
= $1.067 rounded to $1.07

One pint of imported olive oil costs $1.07.

We purchased a kilogram of imported black truffles for $14.00. Our recipe calls for 1 pound of truffles. We weigh out 1 pound and use it. What is the cost of the truffles in our recipe? Use the multiplier that converts pounds to kilograms.

$14.00 (cost for 1 kilogram) × .4536 (multiplier) = $6.35

One pound of truffles cost $6.35.

The conversion process from traditional U.S. units of measure to the metric system units of measure is easy using multipliers. The conversion process for pricing units is easy as well.

## CONVERTING VOLUME TO WEIGHT OR WEIGHT TO VOLUME

Volume measurements are most accurate for liquids, and weight is most accurate for solids. It is not uncommon to find a recipe where the units of measure listed do not clearly follow this rule.

*Corn Bread a la Example*

| | |
|---|---|
| 2 cups corn meal | Corn meal should be weighed |
| 2 ounces oil | 2 fluid ounces of oil, or 1/4 of a cup |
| 1 can corn | Canned corn comes in a variety of sizes and styles. |
| | Do we add the entire can or drain the liquid from the can? |
| 8 ounces milk | 1 cup, unless this is powdered milk |

Some recipes are unclear as to the correct or exact unit of measure. When faced with this situation, we rely on our culinary skills and knowledge and do our best to evaluate which unit of measure makes sense. If we are faced with a recipe that is not correctly written, it is wise to prepare it in a small batch, carefully writing down the changes/adjustments we make. After the recipe is completed, we can evaluate how successful our changing/adjusting was. There are guides in many culinary books that can assist with the changing and adjusting of recipes that are written incorrectly. The guides most often estimate how much a solid item weighs based on a volume unit of measure.

Accurate measurement is critically important to a successful food service operation. Accurate measurement ensures that guests will receive a consistent product each time they order an item from the menu. It also ensures that your portions are consistent and your portion costing and menu pricing is correct.

## UNITS OF MEASURE: REVIEW PROBLEMS

1. Name the volume units of measure used in the United States.

2. Name the metric system volume units of measure.

3. Name the weight units of measure used in the United States.

4. Name the metric system weight units of measure.

5. Why can a multiplier be used to convert between the traditional U.S. units of measure and metric system units of measure?

6. Recipe conversion: A recipe in a French cookbook lists the quantity of whipping cream as 500 mL. You have purchased a quart of whipping cream for $2.39.

   a. Do you have enough whipping cream for this recipe?

   b. Will you have any whipping cream left after using 500 mL?

   c. How much does the quantity 500 mL cost?

7. A recipe in the same French cookbook lists the meat quantity for pâté as 1.5 kilograms. You have 5 pounds of the meat.

   a. How many pounds equal 1.5 kilograms?

   b. Do you have enough meat to make this recipe?

   c. Will there be any leftover meat after the recipe is complete?

   d. The purchase price per pound for the meat was $2.25. How much did it cost for the meat in this recipe?

### Units of Measure: Review Answers

1. Gallon, quart, pint, cup, fluid ounce, tablespoon, teaspoon

2. Liter and milliliter

3. Pound and ounce

4. Kilogram and gram

5. The relationship between the units of measure is constant, it never changes. Therefore, a mathematical relationship can be developed.

6. Recipe conversion:

   a. The recipe uses 500 mL. 1 quart = 946 mL. You have enough whipping cream.

   b. If we use 500 mL, how much will be left? 946 − 500 = 446 mL

   c. Quart costs \$2.39, 946 mL cost \$2.39. \$2.39 / 946 = .0025 per mL

      .0025 × 500 = \$1.25 cost for 500 mL whipping cream

7. a. There are 2.2046 (multiplier) pounds in 1 kilogram.

   2.2046 (pounds per kilogram) × 1.5 (kilograms) = 3.3069 pounds

   b. Yes, you have 5 pounds and the recipe calls for 3.3 pounds.

   c. Yes, there will be 5 (pounds) − 3.3 (pounds) = 1.7 pounds of leftover meat.

   d. \$2.25 (price per pound) × 3.3 (pounds) = \$7.43

Chapter 3

# THE PURCHASING FUNCTION AND ITS RELATIONSHIP TO COST

The purchasing function is critical to a successful food service operation. The decisions made on the type of food purchased and the price paid for the food resonate throughout the entire operation. Every staff member, as well as our clientele, is affected by what and how we purchase.

A food service operation should devote a lot of time and attention to developing a purchasing plan of action and well organized purchasing goals. The goals should include purchasing in the right quality and quantity, getting value for the price, and selecting the best purveyor and timely product delivery.

## QUALITY

Food should be purchased in the quality best suited for its intended use. Almost every food product is available in a variety of forms and quality standards. The decision as to which form or quality standard to purchase is related to the final use of the product. It is not uncommon for a food service operation to purchase the same item in different forms or quality.

Tomatoes are an example of a common product purchased in different forms and quality. One tomato product is ketchup. Ketchup is a staple in a food service operation. Should you purchase a name brand? What are the choices among name-brand ketchup? What about a no-name brand? What are the choices among no-name brands? Should we buy 14-ounce bottles or No. 10 cans? Will the customers complain if the ketchup is not to their liking?

Canned tomatoes can be purchased stewed, crushed, as paste, or diced. Do we need to purchase every type of canned tomato product? Which brand name should we purchase? What can size should we purchase? Is there really a difference between a brand name and a no-name canned tomato product? Is there a way to compare different products to find the best quality for each food service operation?

Fresh tomatoes are also available. A beefsteak tomato is the largest and most expensive fresh tomato. It is used as a center of the plate item. An example is a stuffed beefsteak tomato with a tuna or chicken salad. We also purchase a smaller-size fresh tomato for our dinner salad. The smaller size is cheaper. Should we buy the smaller size and use it for both the stuffed tomato entree and the dinner salad? Would the smaller tomato give the same plate presentation as the beefsteak? Should we use the beefsteak tomato for the dinner salad? How will the decision to change our tomato affect the customers?

The smaller tomato will not deliver the pizzazz to the plate that the beefsteak does. The quality of a beefsteak tomato exceeds what is needed for the dinner salad. Therefore, even though the operation might save some money buying the smaller tomatoes, the best decision is to keep the beefsteak for the stuffed tomato and the smaller tomato for the dinner salad. The decision to purchase different forms and quality of products should be based on the intended use of the product.

## QUANTITY

Many factors affect the quantity of product to order. Some of the most critical factors are usage, type of product (dry good, frozen, or fresh), whether it is a direct or an inventory item, and the delivery schedule of the purveyor.

Usage is the key to order quantity. Any items needed to prepare the static menu offerings must be available when the prep begins. The quantity ordered should be just enough to give the operation adequate inventory until the next delivery arrives. *Adequate* means there is enough product so all of our guests are served and there is a minimum amount of product in inventory when the next order is delivered. The best way to accurately order the proper quantity of food is to establish a par for every item.

A par represents the number of units of a product that we need to have available from the time the product is received until the next delivery arrives. Each item will have a different par level because each product is unique in type and usage. Par levels should be established for every item in the refrigerators, in freezers, and in dry-storage inventory.

Pars are calculated at three different levels: a maximum, a minimum, and an order quantity. Par levels are developed based on the quantity of each item used and the lead time for each item. Lead time is the amount of time it takes for an item to be delivered after it is ordered.

1. *The maximum par level is the greatest number of units of a product in inventory.* The maximum par level is reached as soon as an order is received and put away. The maximum par level represents all of the space we have in storage for each item.
2. *The minimum par level is the number of units that will be available right before an order is received.* When determining a minimum par level, a safety level needs to be considered. A guest should not be disappointed because we have run out of a favorite item. We must ensure that we have enough product to carry us through to the next delivery and consider the fact that a problem can delay the product's arrival.
3. *The order quantity par level represents the exact number of units in inventory when it becomes necessary to place an order.* The order quantity par level is based on daily product usage and lead time. When an item reaches its order quantity par level, an order is placed. When the order is received, the par level goes from minimum to maximum.

Jill's Jungle Juice Bar uses a case of pineapple juice daily. Pineapple juice is delivered every two weeks. Jill uses 7 cases per week, and she has a safety level of 5 cases. Currently, the safety level of 5 cases is inventory. Jill orders 14 cases every two weeks. The lead time for a delivery is one week.

When the order arrives, 14 cases are delivered and added to the safety level in inventory. The maximum par level for pineapple juice is 19 cases.

$$14 \text{ cases} + 5 \text{ cases (safety level)} = 19 \text{ cases}$$

The lead time for a delivery is one week. Jill uses 7 cases in one week. The order quantity par level is 12 cases.

19 cases − 7 cases (weekly usage and lead time) = 12 cases

Seven days will pass before Jill receives another delivery of pineapple juice. Jill uses 1 case of pineapple juice per day. Pineapple juice will be at its minimum level when the new order is received. The minimum par level is 5 cases.

12 cases (order quantity) − 7 cases (lead-time usage) = 5 cases

The pineapple juice in this example is an inventory item. Inventory items are items that are kept in a storeroom because they are used regularly. Inventory is necessary to ensure product availability and because a purveyor will not deliver on a daily basis. Inventory is one of the business's assets and should be thought of as a bank account. The items in inventory are paid for and will generate revenue after they are prepared and sold to our customers.

Because inventory items are paid for after they are received, it is important that we manage the dollar value in inventory. If we place an order that is larger than it needs to be, we are paying more money for inventory than we need to. Profitable food service operators manage their inventory quantities because of cash-flow issues.

At TJ's Taco Shop, the average food cost for inventory items per week is $2,500. This means that TJ should be spending approximately $2,500 per week buying inventory items. If TJ purchased $3,500 worth of food one week, the $1,000 used to pay for excess food products is not available to pay other expenses or for the profit that week.

Inventory items are purchased by the case. New deliveries of inventory items are added to existing inventory once they are received. Par levels are updated. Items in inventory should be organized and new stock properly rotated. The general rule for all food service products is *first in, first out* (FIFO).

*Directs* are food products that are purchased and not placed into inventory. Directs go directly into production. Either these items are very fragile and lose quality if stored or they are not used regularly. The value of a direct is added into the food cost for the day they are delivered.

## ORDERING DRY GOODS

Dry goods are items that are stored at room temperature. Dry-good food products can be canned, in glass bottles, in paper boxes, or in paper or plastic bags. Examples of dry-good food products are a case of cans of chili, a case of bottles of ketchup, a case of boxed cake mix, a 50-pound bag of flour, or a 5-pound bag of rice. Paper products and cleaning chemicals are dry-good items, too. Dry goods are inventory items, and they have a long shelf life. They are purchased either weekly, biweekly, or monthly. A par system is used to determine the correct quantities to order. Dry goods are readily available and do not need to be stockpiled because they are common. However, if there is a discount on the price of an item if a certain volume is purchased, it might make financial sense to buy a larger quantity.

Diced tomatoes are packed six No. 10 cans per case. A case costs $12.00. You use 4 cases per week.

$12.00 (case price) × 4 (weekly case usage) = $48.00

The weekly cost for diced tomatoes is $48.00. This week there is a special on diced tomatoes. If you order 8 cases or more, the case price is $6.00. Normally, you order 4 cases. Should you increase your weekly order?

$6.00 (sale case price) × 4 (weekly case usage) = $24.00

By ordering extra cases this week, you cut your cost for diced tomatoes in half. The extra $24.00 goes directly to your profit.

$48.00 (weekly usage cost) − $24.00 (sale weekly cost)
= $24.00 (weekly savings)

In this instance, it makes sense to increase your order quantity because you can save money on the item and you will use the extra cases in the following weeks.

## ORDERING REFRIGERATED ITEMS

Refrigerated items are stored between 28 and 45°F. The cost of refrigerated storage is a factor to consider because of the cost of the equipment and utilities. Refrigerated items are highly perishable and have a limited shelf life. Due to these facts, refrigerated items are purchased in smaller quantities and delivered more frequently. There are many types of refrigerated food products.

Fresh finfish and seafood are the most perishable refrigerated items. They should be stored at 28°F. Fresh finfish and seafood should be purchased in quantities that match, as closely as possible, its daily usage. Due to the fact that fresh seafood is so perishable, in some situations, it is better to purchase finfish and seafood frozen.

Fresh meats should be stored between 30 and 36°F. Fresh meat has a shelf life of one to five days. Ground meat has the shortest life, while a beef roast has the longest refrigerated shelf life. In some instances, just as with finfish and seafood, it might be better to purchase meat products frozen. Fresh poultry should be stored at 32°F. Fresh poultry has a shelf life of two days. Cooked poultry can be stored up to four days in a refrigerator.

Dairy products are very common in food service. Dairy products should be stored at 38°F. The most perishable dairy items are milk and soft cheeses. Eggs, hard cheese, and butter have a longer shelf life. Par levels need to be developed for dairy items. Once this is accomplished, the dairy delivery person will bring the stock levels up to par several times weekly.

Fresh produce is stored at 45°F. There are so many different types of fresh produce products that it is difficult to make any type of generalization. Some items can last for a weeks if temperature and humidity levels are controlled. Other items, such as fresh raspberries, have a very limited shelf life. Order quantities need to take into account the perishability of the product and the delivery schedule of the purveyor.

## ORDERING FROZEN ITEMS

Frozen foods need to be stored at 0°F or below. Although most perishable food products have a longer shelf life when frozen, the quality of the product is affected. The longer a product is kept in a frozen state, the more the quality suffers. Frozen foods must be properly wrapped in order to ensure product quality. Freezer space is expensive because of the cost of equipment and the utility expense.

Frozen food items should have par levels that reflect usage and purveyor delivery schedules. Frozen food items are easy to forget about so it is in the best financial interest of a food service operation to properly manage freezer inventory.

## VALUE/PRICE RELATIONSHIP

Customers select a food service operation based on service, sanitation, food quality, and value. Everyone perceives value differently. Value for the food service customer means the menu price is equal to the quality of service and food.

Value, for the food service operator, means buying the best product for its intended use at the best possible price. The best product is not necessarily the highest quality or the most expensive. The best product is the one that is suitable for the final product and is within a certain price range.

*Specifications* are the first step in developing a purchasing program that offers value to the food service operator. A specification describes the product needed using information that is generally accepted and understood by the food service industry. A specification needs to describe a product in enough detail that multiple purveyors understand which item or items fit the description. Specifications are sent to a number of purveyors to compare the price quoted for the same or a comparable product.

A specification should include the item name, quality, brand, form, the unit that the price is based on, and other miscellaneous information to ensure that the correct product is ordered. A specification for pineapple juice might look like this:

*Specification Form*

| | |
|---|---|
| Item: | Pineapple Juice |
| Quality: | Brand name or generic product |
| Form: | 46-oz. cans, 12 per case |
| Price per unit: | can or case |

Price is not always the best indicator of value. A great price on milk that is out of date tomorrow is not good value unless you can use all of the milk by its expiration date. The best value in dairy products is the freshest product available, provided it is priced competitively.

In addition to the quoted price for the food product(s), there are other factors to consider. Most purveyors will only deliver if a minimum quantity of product or a certain dollar value is ordered.

Some food service operators may find it difficult to meet the minimum order if they attempt to "cherry-pick." This means they shop price from many different purveyors. If we place small orders based on the best price from each vendor, we might have to pay for delivery or pick up the products ourselves. The cost of the delivery or the cost of picking up the products needs to be considered in the total product cost. Time is a valuable commodity as well. If we find a purveyor—supplier—who offers all or a majority of the products we need and buying from one location saves us several hours a month, then there is some value to purchasing from that purveyor.

## VALUE ADDED

*Value added* means that as the food product passes through the processing channels, it becomes a more valuable or a more expensive commodity. If you were looking for the best price on fresh strawberries, you would need to drive to a "pick-your-own" strawberry farm. There you would be able to buy berries cheaper than anywhere else. However, the time invested in the drive to pick the berries needs to be considered. When a delivery person drops off strawberries at your back door, even though they cost more than the farm price, there is value added for the convenience of the delivery.

Some products are labor intensive. If we purchase unshelled shrimp, someone in our kitchens will need to shell and devein the shrimp before we can use them. If we purchase shelled and deveined shrimp, the price per pound is higher, but the product is recipe ready. There is thus value added to the shelled and deveined shrimp. If you have employees that have free time, then it is wise to purchase the unshelled product. If your employees are too busy to shell the shrimp, it is wise to purchase the value-added product.

## PURVEYOR SELECTION

The selection of a food and supplies purveyor is the foundation of a business relationship that hopefully is beneficial to both parties. A reputable supplier can enhance the ability of a food service operation to offer value to its customers and to earn a profit. The purveyor earns a reputation by providing a variety of products and services necessary for the food service operator. An ethical food purveyor will offer value and information on new products, pass on "good" buys to their clients, have a clean and sanitary warehouse, and deliver products before they are needed.

Most food service operations have a number of purveyors they can decide to do business with. If you have selected a purveyor who does not meet your expectations, then you need to change to one that can. The food that we offer for sale to our customers is only as good as the food the purveyor delivers.

## PRODUCT DELIVERY

The convenience of product delivery cannot be overstated. A good delivery person will arrive at the loading dock at a time that is convenient for the food service operation to check the products and to receive them. A good delivery person will deliver the correct products in the correct quantity. If there is a problem, they will fix it. Once the products are inspected and signed for, we are legally liable to pay for them. A good driver will make sure we pay for the products we ordered.

## THE AUDIT TRAIL

A *purchase order* (PO) is created every time we order food. The purchase order lists each item ordered, the quantity ordered, and the price per unit. Items can be priced by the case, by the pound, or by the each.

A purchase order is a document produced in triplicate. One copy is sent to the purveyor, one copy is given to the receiving area, and one copy goes to accounts payable. As the goods are delivered, the receiver checks the items delivered to ensure they match the items ordered on the purchase order. If the items delivered match the purchase order, the delivery person has the receiver sign the invoice. The invoice is a document in triplicate. Once signed, the delivery person leaves one copy with the receiver. The two remaining copies are returned to the purveyors for their accounting department.

The signed invoice received from the delivery person is a binding legal document. Once the receiver signs the invoice, that confirms that we have received the goods and the legal ownership of the goods is transferred from the purveyor to the food service operation. At that point, we are liable for payment.

Once the food is received, our copy of the invoice is sent to the accounts payable office. The accounts payable personnel check the

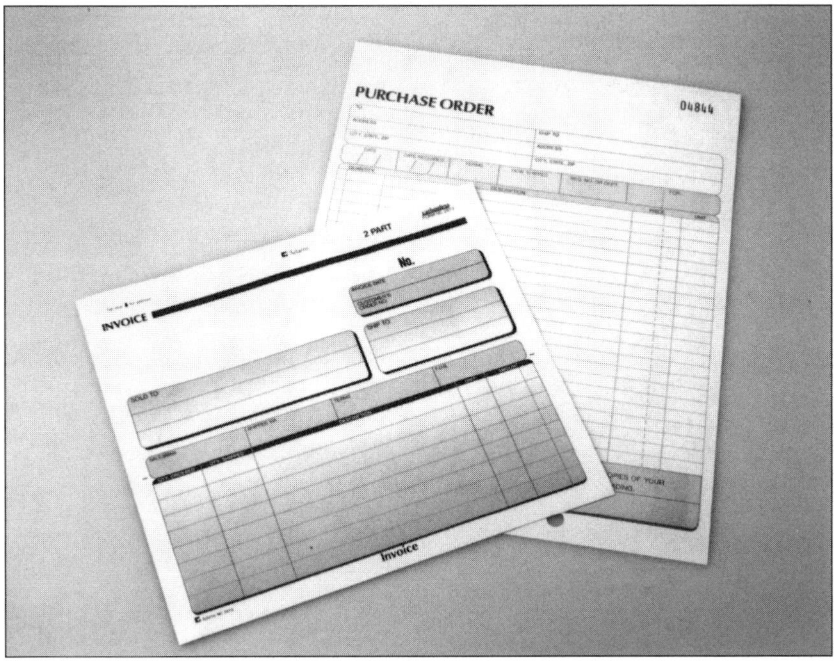


**FIGURE 3.1** Invoice and Purchase Order forms. Photography by Thomas Myers.

invoice against the purchase order. They check to see if the quantity ordered and the price per unit is correct. If it is, the invoice is processed for payment. The price we agreed to pay for each product becomes the foundation of our food cost.

## AS-PURCHASED, EDIBLE-PORTION, AND AS-SERVED YIELDS

When food is purchased, it is commonly delivered in a form or state that is very different from the finished product that will be served to our guests. For example, if we purchase a prime rib roast, it can arrive at our loading dock either fresh or frozen. The roast can weigh 10 pounds. Before we can serve our guests prime rib, we must cook the roast. After the roast comes out of the oven, it needs to stand for 15 to 30 minutes. Then we can slice the roast into the portion size that we serve to our guests.

We use different terms to identify the various stages in food production from purchasing to serving. When we buy the roast, we receive a piece of beef that has a certain weight at a certain price per pound. This is known as the *as-purchased* weight and price. We commonly call this *AP.*

After the roast is cooked and is taken out of the oven, it is now edible. The entire roast at this point is called the *edible portion.* The edible portion is commonly called the *EP.* The edible portion has a weight and a price per pound that is different than the AP weight and price per pound due to possible trimming and/or cooking loss. The entire edible portion of the roast may not be able to be served to the guest for various reasons. The most common reason is that our portion size does not divide equally into the edible portion. If this is the case, we have some edible product that cannot be sold, and this will affect our final portion cost.

The prime rib roast is then sliced into the portion size that is served to the guest. The portion is called *as served.* The as-served portion is commonly called *AS.* The AS weight and cost is the portion size and the portion cost of the product we serve to the guest.

In some circumstances, the EP weight and price is equal to the AS weight and price, EP = AS. Others times, the EP weight and price is not equal to the AS weight and price, EP ≠ AS. Factors that affect the relationship of EP to AS are the portion size, the final presentation of the product, and the loss in cutting, trimming, slicing, or carving.

As the prime rib roast goes through the cycle from purchasing to serving, it changes. The most dramatic change is in the weight of the item. It is possible that the 10-pound prime rib that we purchased may only serve 16 guests an 8-ounce portion. Let's compare

**FIGURE 3.2** Prime rib roast, total edible portion (EP) and as-served (AS) portion.
Photography by Thomas Myers.

the number of 8-ounce portions that we could slice from the 10-pound AP prime rib versus the amount that we were able to serve from the cooked EP prime rib. For this example, EP = AS.

A 10-pound prime rib roast weighs 160 ounces:

10 (pounds) × 16 (ounces per pound) = 160 ounces

How many 8-ounce portions can we serve from 160 ounces?

160 (ounces) / 8 (ounces) = 20 (8-ounce portions)

But we were able to serve only sixteen 8-ounce portions after we cooked the prime rib roast.

How many ounces of EP/AS prime rib did we have if we could serve only 16 portions?

16 (8-ounce portions) × 8 (ounces per portion) = 128 ounces

We were left with 128 ounces EP/AS of prime rib from an AP prime rib roast of 160 ounces. How many pounds of prime rib did we had to serve?

128 (ounces) / 16 (ounces per pound) = 8 pounds

We began with an AP prime rib roast at 10 pounds and finished with an EP/AS prime rib roast at 8 pounds. The difference between the original AP weight and the EP weight or the AS weight is called the *yield.* Yield is the amount of food product available after the preparation and cooking process. It is the amount of product available to serve the guest. In addition to the yield, we end up with a yield percentage.

The *yield percentage* describes the relationship between the AP product and the EP or AS product. In order to determine the yield percentage, we need to divide.

$$\text{Yield percentage} = \frac{\text{EP } or \text{ AS weight}}{\text{Original weight}}$$

The yield percentage for our sample prime rib roast is

8 pounds (EP/AS weight) / 10 pounds (AP weight) = .80, or 80%

*or*

128 ounces (EP/AS weight) / 160 ounces (AP weight) = .80, or 80%

The yield percentage tells us that we have available for sale only 80 percent of the weight of the AP prime rib roast. In this example, the roast has a 20 percent weight loss due to trimming and shrinkage during the cooking process. The yield percentage gives us valuable information. This information affects the actual cost of the food we serve to our guests and the amount of food product we need to purchase. Let us continue with the prime rib roast example to illustrate these points.

The AP prime rib roast weighed 10 pounds. We paid $2.00 per pound AP. The total cost for the AP 10-pound roast was $20.00.

10 pounds × $2.00 per pound = $20.00

We serve an 8-ounce portion of prime rib to our guests. The portion cost for 8-ounces from our AP weight and price, would be

10 pounds × 16 (ounces per pound) = 160 ounces

160 ounces / 8 (ounces per portion) = 20 (8-ounce portions)

$20.00 (total AP cost) / 20 (number of 8-ounce portions) = $1.00 (AP cost per portion)

The problem is, we were not able to serve 20 portions due to trimming and shrinkage. We were able to serve only 16 portions. So how much was our actual portion cost?

The AP price for the roast remains the same, \$20.00, but the AP weight of the product is reduced.

AP price = EP or AS price    AP weight > EP or AS weight

8 pounds (EP or AS weight) × 16 (ounces per pound)
= 128 ounces

128 ounces / 8 (ounces per portion) = 16 (8-ounce portions)

\$20.00 (total AP cost) / 16 (number of 8-ounce portions)
= \$1.25 EP or AS cost per portion

The true cost for an 8-ounce portion of prime rib is \$1.25, *not* \$1.00. Every food product that has a yield variance between AP weight and EP or AS weight, also has a *price* variance between AP price and EP or AS price.

There are different mathematical methods we can use to obtain this price information. The quickest and easiest way is to use the yield percentage. It works like this:

$$\text{EP or AS price} = \frac{\text{AP price}}{\text{Yield percentage}}$$

$$\text{EP or AS price} = \frac{\$2.00 \text{ (price per pound for the roast)}}{.80}$$

\$2.50 is the EP or AS price per pound

\$2.50 (price per pound) / 16 (ounces per pound)
= \$0.15625 rounded to \$0.16 per ounce

\$0.16 (price per ounce) × 8 (ounces per portion)
= \$1.28 (price per 8-ounce portion)

\$1.28 is the EP or AS price per portion

*or*

\$2.50 / 2 (there are two 8-ounce portions in one pound)
= \$1.25 (rounding accounts for the difference in totals)

Price is not the only factor affected by a yield variance. The quantity of food we need to purchase is also affected by a yield variance. As the AP weight of a food product shrinks, so do the number of guests we can serve from the AP product. This means we must purchase a greater quantity of product to compensate for the loss of product.

We are serving prime rib to a group of 20 guests. How many AP pounds of prime rib do we need to purchase to have 20 EP or AS portions?

$$20 \text{ (portions)} \times 8 \text{ (ounces per portion)} = 160 \text{ ounces}$$

$$160 \text{ ounces} / 16 \text{ (ounces per pound)} = 10 \text{ EP or AS pounds}$$

We need to have 10 pounds of prime rib EP or AS. Our yield percentage is .80, or 80 percent. We need to purchase a quantity greater than 10 pounds, but, how much do we need to purchase? If we divide our AS weight by our yield percentage, the answer will tell us how many pounds of AP prime rib we need to purchase.

$$\text{Quantity to purchase} = \frac{10 \text{ pounds (EP or AS needed)}}{.80}$$

$$\text{Quantity to purchase} = 12.5 \text{ pounds}$$

The AP weight of a prime rib roast to serve 20 guests an 8-ounce portion is 12.5 pounds. The AP weight of 12.5 pounds yields an EP or AS weight of 10 pounds. How much will it cost to serve 20 guests?

$$\$2.00 \text{ (AP price per pound)} \times 12.5 \text{ (AP pounds)} = \$25.00$$

*or*

$$\$20.00 \text{ (AP price for 10 pounds)} / .80 = \$25.00$$

The determination of the yield variance and its subsequent use to determine the actual portion cost and the correct quantity to purchase is critical to running a successful food service operation.

## THE PURCHASING FUNCTION AND ITS RELATIONSHIP TO COST: REVIEW PROBLEMS

1. Why is the purchasing function so important to a food service operation?

2. What does *quality* mean?

3. What does the *best quality for its intended use* mean?

4. How do we determine the correct order quantity?

5. What is *value* to a food service operator?

6. What does *value added* mean to a food service operator?

7. Why do we have an *audit trail*?

8. What does AP mean?

9. What does EP mean?

10. What does AS mean?

11. What is the difference between EP and AS?

12. What is a *yield percentage*?

### Maximum, Minimum, and Order-Quantity Par Levels

13. The Lucky Luau uses a large quantity of canned pineapple rings. The Lucky Luau is open seven days each week.

| | |
|---|---|
| Product: | canned pineapple rings |
| Purchase Unit: | case |
| Usage Rate: | 3 cases per day |
| Lead Time: | 2 days |
| Safety Level: | 3 days |

a. What is the weekly usage rate?
(# of cases used per day × 7 days)

b. What is the lead-time usage rate?
(lead time in days × usage rate per day)

c. What quantity constitutes a safety level?
(safety level in days × usage per day)

d. What is the order point par level?
(lead-time quantity + safety level)

e. What is the maximum inventory level?
(weekly usage rate + safety level)

f. What is the minimum inventory level?
(Order point − lead-time quantity)

**As Purchased (AP), Edible Portion (EP), As Served (AS)**

**14.** Alan's All-Night Drive-Thru serves "The Best Roast Beef Sandwich in Town." Alan serves 200 sandwiches every weekend. There are 4 ounces of roast beef on every sandwich.

a. Alan has received a new roast-beef product. The AP weight is 16 pounds. After the roast is cooked, the EP weight is 13 pounds. What is the yield percentage?

b. If the AP price per pound is $1.59, what is the EP price per pound?

c. If the AP price per pound is $1.98, what is the EP price per pound?

d. How many pounds of EP roast beef does Alan need each weekend?

e. How many AP pounds of roast beef does Alan need to purchase?

**15.** Alan decided to add tacos to his all-night menu. He will serve a 2-ounce portion of cooked ground beef per taco shell. He estimates that he will serve 100 tacos over the weekend.

a. How many pounds of EP ground beef will Alan need for 100 tacos?

b. Alan has a choice of two ground-beef combinations. Which item offers the best value?

| *Item A* | *Item B* |
|---|---|
| Product: ground beef | Product: ground beef |
| Purchase unit: pound | Purchase unit: pound |
| Price per pound: $1.59 | Price per pound: $1.89 |
| Yield: 78% | Yield: 90% |

c. How many pounds of each of these ground beef items would Alan need to purchase to serve 100 tacos?

## The Purchasing Function and Its Relationship to Cost: Review Answers

**1.** The purchasing function determines the type of food, the quality of food, the cost of food, the cash flow of our operation, the menu price, and the type of customer we serve.

**2.** *Quality* means a degree or grade of excellence. In food service, quality is determined by industry standards.

**3.** The *best quality for its intended use* means that every product we purchase is used in a different way and the quality we need varies by intended use.

**4.** The correct order quantity is determined by delivery schedules, usage between deliveries, and storage space available. Once the correct order quantities are determined, we establish multiple *par levels* for each inventory item.

5. *Value* to a food service operator is purchasing the best-quality products for their intended use at the best overall price.

6. *Value added* means that the product is delivered to the food service operation in a form or state that requires less labor to get the product recipe ready.

7. An audit trail is a financial control vehicle. It allows us to track our purchasing costs and to ensure we receive and pay for the products we indeed purchased.

8. AP means as purchased.

9. EP means edible portion.

10. AS means as served.

11. The difference between EP and AS is that the entire edible portion of a product may or may not be able to be served to our guests. It depends on the type of product, the portion size, and the plate presentation of the product.

12. A *yield percentage* is a decimal or a percentage that represents the variance between the AP weight of a product and its EP or AS weight.

### Maximum, Minimum, and Order-Quantity Par Levels

13. a. 21 cases
    b. 6 cases
    c. 9 cases
    d. 15 cases
    e. 30 cases
    f. 9 cases

### As Purchased (AP), Edible Portion (EP), As Served (AS)

14. a. Yield percentage = EP weight / AP weight
    = 13/16
    = .8125, or 81.25%

b. EP price per pound

= AP price per pound / Yield percentage

= $1.59 / .8125

= $1.96 per pound

c. EP = $1.98 / .8125

= $2.44 per pound

d. 200 sandwiches × 4 oz. = 800 oz.

800 oz. / 16 = 50 EP pounds

e. AP weight = EP weight / yield percentage

= 50 / .8125

= 61.5 AP pounds

**15.** a. 100 × 2 oz = 200 oz

200 / 16 = 12.5 EP pounds

b. Item A $1.59/ .78 = $2.04 per pound

Item B $1.89 / .90 = $2.10 per pound

c. Item A 12.5 pounds/ .78 = 16 pounds

Item B 12.5 pounds/ .90 = 13.9, or 14 pounds

# Chapter 4
# FOOD-PRODUCT GROUPS

## CENTER-OF-THE-PLATE ITEMS WITH A HIGH FOOD COST

Food service operations purchase a wide variety of products. Every product group has unique characteristics. Product groups react differently with respect to yield; yield percentage; AP, EP, and AS weight; and price. The critical issue to understand is that a food-product group's yield behavior has a dramatic effect on the plate cost of the menu items we serve to our guests. Let's review the major food-product groups so we can see the effect of yield on the plate cost.

### Meats

Meats include beef, veal/calf, pork, and lamb. The animals that supply our meat products are bulls, cows, pigs, and sheep. All meat-producing animals are butchered in a similar fashion. Beef and sheep carcasses are evaluated based on yield and quality. Yield grades are No. 1 to No. 5, with a yield grade No.1 yielding more usable meat than a yield grade No. 5. Beef-quality grades used in food service are prime, choice, select, and standard, with prime the most flavorful and most expensive quality grade. Sheep-quality grades used in food service are prime, choice, and good.

Veal/calf carcasses are only graded for quality. The quality grades are the same as beef. Pork carcasses are only graded on yield. The evaluation is based on the quality of the meat. The yield grades are No. 1 to No. 4, with the highest yield grade a No. 1.

Meats can be purchased in a variety of forms. The forms vary from a whole carcass to a side of meat, a quarter of a side or a primal cut to a portion-controlled hamburger patty. The processing of the animals has become extremely efficient and has affected the forms of meat we purchase. It is unusual today to purchase a whole carcass or a side of meat. The cost of on-site butchering for these large pieces of meat along with the increased cost of transportation makes it cost-effective to purchase smaller units of meat. The smaller units are generally a primal cut, an oven-ready or a portion-controlled unit, sold by the pound and shipped and delivered in a manageable-size cardboard box.

When meat is purchased, it is priced by the pound. The larger forms of meat, whole carcass, side, quarter or primal cuts, are less expensive per pound than an oven-ready or portion-controlled unit. However, the form, yield grade, and quality grade purchased, along with the cooking method, will have a dramatic effect on the product's yield percentage and AS price per portion.

Meats purchased by the carcass, side, quarter, or primal cut will have a precooking yield variance. Meat purchased in one of these forms must be cut and trimmed into a usable end product to serve to guests. The process of cutting and trimming cuts off bone and fat, reduces the original purchase weight. Meat purchased in these forms is trimmed into roasts or steaks, with the byproducts used as tips, stew meat, ground meat, or stock. The AP price per pound for one of these forms is less than the AP price per pound for an oven-

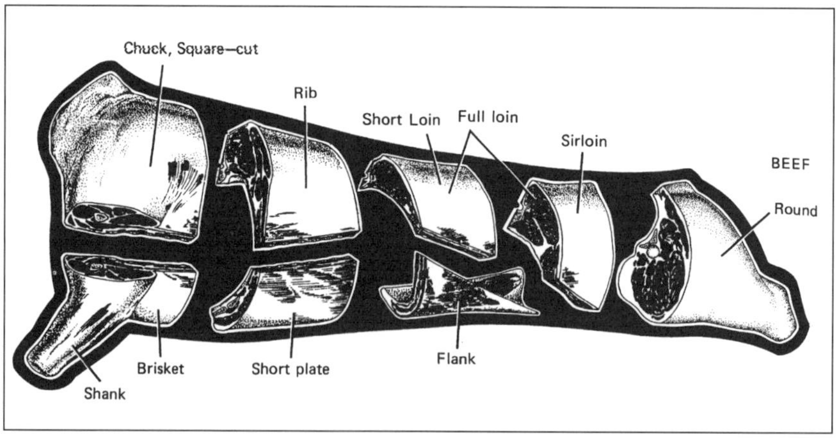


**FIGURE 4.1** Beef cuts. Courtesy National Live Stock and Meat Board. © Cattlemen's Beef Board & National Cattlemen's Beef Association.

ready roast or a portion-controlled product. The reason for the price difference is the the cost of labor associated with on-site cutting and trimming and the loss of AP weight.

Therefore, when purchasing a meat item by the carcass, side, quarter, or primal cut, the following relationship occurs:

AP price per pound < EP or AS price per pound

AP weight > EP or AS weight

A similar scenario exists when we purchase meat in the form of a roast. Many roasts will need some trimming before they are placed in the oven to cook. Every time we trim a roast, we are taking away AP weight. Moreover, shrinkage occurs as part of the cooking process.

Therefore, when purchasing meat as a roast, the following relationship occurs:

AP price per pound < EP or AS price per pound

AP weight > EP or AS weight

The prime rib roast example in Chapter 3 on purchasing explains how both AP weight and price change as we arrive at the EP and AS weight and price for meat.

Meat can also be purchased in portion-cut units. Portion-cut meats are trimmed before we receive them. Each unit has a specific weight. Portion-cut steaks can weigh from 3 ounces to 1 pound. Portion-cut hamburger patties can weigh from 4 ounces (1/4, 25 percent, or .25 of a pound) to 8 ounces (1/2, 50 percent, or .50 of a pound). Portion-cut meats are priced by the pound.

*Portion-cut* means we purchase the product at a precooking weight that we will serve to our guest; therefore, with portion-cut meats:

EP = AS

Portion-cut meats, like any meat product, shrink during the cooking process. Therefore,

AP weight > EP or AS weight

Portion-cut meats are purchased by the pound but are often served by the ounce. The way we determine the portion cost is based on the per-pound cost. If a case of 8-ounce steaks costs $3.30 per pound, how much is each 8-ounce portion?

$3.30 (cost per pound) / 16 (number of ounces in a pound)
= $0.20625 per ounce

$0.20625 (cost per ounce) × 8 (number of ounces per portion)
= $1.65 (cost per 8-ounce portion)

*or*

If we realize that 8 ounces is equal to 1/2, .50, or 50% of a pound:

$3.30 (cost per pound) × (1/2, .50, or 50%) = $1.65

The relationship of AP price per portion to EP or AS price per portion is

AP price per portion = EP or AS price per portion

**Equivalent Price for Meat** At Tina Marie's Meat Menagerie, Tina has many choices when she purchases meat products to serve to her customers. Tina knows that the grade and the form of meat she purchases will affect the price per pound. Tina also knows that as the price per pound for a certain form of meat changes, the actual EP or AS price per pound for two different forms can be equal or equivalent.

Tina can purchase meat in a primal cut, which is trimmed at her restaurant. Purchasing meat by the primal cut is one way to pay a lower price per pound, but the trimming of the primal will result in a substantial yield variance. Tina wants to compare the price per pound of a rib primal to the price per pound of a rib roast so she collects the following information.

A rib, primal, from a small bull averages 26 pounds. A rib roast from the same size animal averages 18 pounds. Therefore, the average yield from a rib primal compared to a rib roast from a small bull is

$$\frac{\text{18 pounds (rib, roast)}}{\text{26 pounds (rib, primal)}} = .69, \text{ or } 69\%$$

Using this information Tina can compare the price per pound of a rib primal to a rib roast. If the price per pound of the rib primal is $1.89 and the trimming yield is .69, or 69 percent, what is the rib roast price-per-pound equivalent?

$1.89 (AP price per pound for a rib primal)
/ .69 (yield % as a decimal)
= $2.74 (equivalent AP price for a rib roast)

Tina can now compare the equivalent AP price per pound for the rib primal of $1.89 to the AP price per pound for a rib roast of $2.74. If Tina can purchase a rib roast for $2.74 per pound, it is an equivalent price per pound to the rib primal at $1.89 per pound. If the price per pound for a rib roast is < $2.74, it is now cheaper for Tina to purchase the rib roast. This example illustrates the equivalent price of the rib primal to the rib roast.

**Multiplier for Price** Tina has just calculated the equivalent price for a rib primal to a rib roast. It is possible that the AP price per pound for both of these items will fluctuate each time Tina makes a purchase. Tina can continue to make her cost comparison by dividing by the yield percentage for these two items, or Tina can develop a multiplier that expresses the relationship between the AP price for each type of rib product.

The AP price for the rib primal has changed to $2.09 a pound. Tina wants to figure the equivalent rib roast AP price.

$2.09 (new AP price for primal) / .69 (yield % as a decimal)
= $3.03 (new equivalent AP price per pound for a rib roast)

*or*

Tina can try something new. She can develop a multiplier using the original AP prices of $1.89 for the rib primal and its equivalent $2.74 for the rib roast. The multiplier expresses this relationship.

Equivalent AP price per pound for the Rib, Roast
/ AP price per pound for the Rib, Primal

$2.74 (equivalent AP price for roast) / $1.89 (AP price for primal)
= 1.4497 multiplier

Now Tina can multiply the new AP price per pound for the rib primal by the multiplier:

$2.09 (new AP price per pound for primal) × 1.4497 (multiplier)
= $3.03 new equivalent AP price per pound for the rib roast)

**Yield Test** When a rib primal is trimmed, the trimmings can be used. Let's take the example of a rib primal from the small bull that has an average weight of 26 pounds and perform a yield test. A yield test compares the type and quantity of usable product available from the trimmings of a piece of meat to the current market price for each type of usable product.

As the rib primal is trimmed, the following products and their weight are produced:

15 pounds rib, roast
3.5 pounds of stew beef
2.5 pounds of short ribs
2.5 pounds of beef bones

Now we need to compare the AP price for the rib primal to the current AP price of the items produced by the trimming of the primal. The current AP prices for this example are as follows:

| | |
|---|---|
| Rib, primal | $1.89 per pound |
| Rib, roast | $2.89 per pound |
| Stew beef | $2.39 per pound |
| Short ribs | $1.79 per pound |
| Beef bones | $0.59 per pound |

The entire rib primal weighs 26 pounds and the AP price is $1.89 per pound. The total cost of the rib primal is

26 (pounds) × $1.89 (price per pound) = $49.14

The total value of the rib roast cut from the primal is

15 (pounds) × $2.89 (current AP price) = $43.35

The total value of the stew beef cut from the primal is

3.5 (pounds) × $2.39 (current AP price) = $8.37

The total value of the short ribs cut from the primal is

2.5 (pounds) × $1.79 (current AP price) = $4.48

The total value of the beef bones cut from the primal is

2.5 (pounds) × $0.59 (current AP price) = $1.48

The total current AP value of the rib primal trimmed is:

$43.35 (rib roast) + $8.37 (stew beef) + $4.48 (short ribs) + $1.48 (beef bones) = $57.68

Let's compare the current AP value of the rib primal trimmed ($57.68) to the AP cost of the rib primal ($49.14):

$57.68 (rib primal, trimmed value)
− $49.14 (AP cost of rib primal) = $8.54

In this scenario the value of the rib primal trimmed is higher than the AP cost of the rib primal by $8.54. So the face value of the comparison might lead Tina Marie to believe that it is cheaper to buy the rib primal and trim it than to buy the rib roast. However, other factors need to be considered.

The first is the expertise to trim the primal. Is Tina Marie, the owner, or any employee qualified to trim the primal? If the answer is yes, then the cost of labor needs to be considered. How much time does it take for Tina Marie or the employee to trim the primal? Do they have the time available in their normal work schedule or does it create the need for additional work hours? Is the cost of labor greater than (>) or less than (<) the cost savings of $8.54?

One further consideration is if there is a use for the other items gained from the trimming of the primal. Do we regularly use stew beef, short ribs, and beef bones? If the answer is yes, then the primal might indeed be the correct meat item to purchase. If the answer is no, purchasing the primal is probably not a cost-effective alternative to purchasing the rib roast.

## Poultry

Chicken, turkey, duck, goose, and game birds are poultry. Game birds include guinea fowl and hen, pigeon, partridge, pheasant, and quail. The federal grades for poultry are A, B, and C with Grade A the highest and most expensive poultry item. Chicken is the most commonly used type of poultry. I would venture to guess that 99 percent of food service operations have a chicken item on their menu.

All poultry can be purchased whole carcass. Some types of poultry are available in pieces—for example, a turkey breast, chicken wings, or in a variety of portion-cut units. When offering poultry items on a menu, many scenarios exist. The whole carcass can be roasted and then cut into pieces for service. The whole carcass can be roasted and then sliced into portions for service. The entire carcass can be served as a portion-cut unit. We can purchase "parts" and serve them as a portion-cut unit.

When poultry is purchased whole carcass, generally it is roasted. The weight of the carcass shrinks during the roasting process. If the carcass is carved, sliced, and portioned, the carving and slicing of the carcass can eliminate the bones. The shrinkage, carving, and slicing of the carcass creates a yield variance. Therefore:

$$\text{AP weight} > \text{EP or AS weight}$$

As the carcass is trimmed, the amount of usable product is determined. There are many variations when serving poultry. The breast meat from a turkey is sliced for service. The wings and legs are served with the bone. Chicken breasts can be served with the bone or boneless. When we purchase a whole carcass it is priced per pound. As we cook and carve the carcass, we lose weight. Therefore:

$$\text{AP price per pound} < \text{EP or AS price per pound}$$

**Example from Chicken Restaurant** Chickens can be purchased whole carcass, halves, quarters, or in 8, 9, or 10 pieces. The processing of chickens is very efficient. Therefore, purchasing a carcass already cut is not too much more expensive than purchasing the carcass whole and cutting it on site. When a chicken is purchased whole carcass, in halves, or 8, 9, or 10 ways, it is priced by the pound. This type of pricing leads us to believe that every part of the carcass has the same value. This is not correct.

The breast of a chicken is white meat, and the white meat is considered the healthiest part. This nutritional benefit gives the chicken breast greater value. The breast also has an excellent center-of-the-plate presentation. The price per pound for chicken breasts can be double, triple, or higher than the price per pound of a whole chicken.

Chicken wings and drummettes are a popular menu item. The price per pound for chicken wings and drummettes is at least 1.5 times that of a whole chicken. The value for the leg quarter (thigh and leg) is the lowest of all the parts of the chicken that are served to guests. The neck, back, and bones carry little value, although they are excellent for flavor development.

The differing values of the different parts of the chicken is an example of how consumer demand for a certain item affects the price. When chicken breasts and wings were not popular menu items, their price per pound was far less than it is today.

Let's use the example of Johnny G's Famous Spicy Barbeque Chicken Restaurant. Johnny serves half a chicken with his famous spicy barbeque sauce. Johnny purchases whole chickens and slowly roasts them is a special mesquite-fired oven. When the chickens are cooked, Johnny slices them in half, at the breast, lays them flat, and

**FIGURE 4.2** Chicken, whole and quartered.
Photography by Thomas Myers.

cuts out the backbone. Then he covers them with his famous sauce and serves them. His yield is two servings per chicken. Each time Johnny purchases a chicken, he is really purchasing two portions.

Chickens are priced by the pound. If the average chicken weighs 3.5 AP pounds and sells for \$0.99 per pound, then, on average, Johnny pays:

3.5 pounds (average AP weight) × \$0.99 (cost per pound)
= \$3.47 per chicken

Johnny purchases two portions for an average cost of \$3.47, or a per-portion cost of

\$3.47 (average cost per chicken)
/ 2 (number of portions per chicken)
= \$1.73 (cost per portion)

The relationship that this scenario presents is

AP weight > EP or AS weight

EP weight = AS weight

AP price per chicken = 2 times the portion cost

*or*

1/2 the AP price per chicken = cost of one portion

Johnny has received several guest comments about his portions being too large. Some of the comment cards asked if he could reduce his portion sizes. Johnny decides to offer a "quarter chicken" special to see if there is demand for a reduced portion. Johnny is offering a choice of the breast quarter (breast and wing) or the leg quarter (thigh and leg). Johnny prepares and roasts the chicken the same. When the special is ordered, the customer may select the breast quarter or the leg portion.

The special obviously has a different portion cost, because we can now serve twice as many portions from each chicken. Using the same information we did for the half chicken, how much is the portion cost for the special?

The average chicken costs \$3.47, but now we can serve four portions from each carcass. The portion cost for a quarter of a chicken is

\$3.47 (average cost per chicken)
/ 4 (number of portions per chicken) = \$0.87*

*or*

\$1.73 (cost per 1/2 chicken portion)
/ 2 (number of portions in 1/2 chicken) = \$0.87*
(* rounded to \$0.87)

**Price Comparison** Johnny has noticed something interesting as he sells his quarter-chicken specials. Johnny finds he is selling more breast quarters than leg quarters. Johnny decides to ask his salesperson how much it costs per pound to purchase breast quarters. Johnny is shocked when his salesperson comes back with a price per pound for breast quarters of \$1.89. Johnny says, "I only pay \$0.99 per pound for the entire chicken. Why is the breast quarter almost twice as much?"

The salesperson explains to Johnny that the breast meat is the "premium" part of the chicken carcass and, therefore, is the most expensive form when purchased separately. Johnny realizes that by buying the whole carcass and cutting the chicken into quarters, he actually can add value to his purchase.

The value comes in when the breast quarter he cuts from the whole chicken has a greater price per pound or cost than the price per pound for the whole chicken. When Johnny prints new menus, he adds the quarter-chicken special as a static menu item, but he is unsure how to price the menu for the breast quarter and the leg quarter. Should the quarter-chicken special, breast and leg, have the same menu price, or should the breast quarter sell for a higher price?

Johnny has always bought chickens whole and cut them up and because the different parts of the chicken have a different value:

AP price per pound of chicken breast
> AP price per pound of whole chicken

Johnny attempts to figure out if he is saving money by buying a whole chicken and cutting it up, as opposed to buying the quarter chicken parts already cut. Johnny calls his poultry purveyor and receives the following information:

| | |
|---|---|
| Whole chicken, average 3.5 pounds | $0.99 per pound |
| Breast quarter | $1.89 per pound |
| Leg quarter | $0.89 per pound |

Then Johnny figures out how much of the whole carcass is actually a salable product as a part of his quarter-chicken menu item. Johnny comes up with the following yield information:

The two breast quarters are 40.3 percent of the whole chicken. The two leg quarters are 27.6 percent of the whole chicken.

40.3% (breast quarters) + 27.6% (leg quarters)
= 67.9% (total usable yield)

The two usable yield from a whole chicken is 67.9 percent. If Johnny pays $0.99 AP per pound for a whole chicken and the yield is 67.9 percent, then the EP price per pound is

$0.99 (AP price per pound) / .679 (yield percentage as a decimal)
= $1.46 (EP price per pound)

When Johnny buys a whole chicken and cuts it up for his quarter-chicken special, he actually pays $1.46 per pound for the EP and AS pieces. In this example, EP = AS.

An AP 3.5-pound chicken weighs 56 ounces.

3.5 (pounds) × 16 (ounces per pound) = 56 ounces

The breast quarters are 40.3 percent of the whole carcass. If a whole chicken weighs, on average, 3.5 pounds, then the breast quarters weigh

56 ounces × .403 (breast quarters as a decimal)
= 22.57 ounces of breast on a 3.5-pound carcass

*or*

22.57 ounces / 16 (ounces in a pound)
= 1.41 pounds of breast quarters

*or*

.403 (breast quarters as a decimal)
× 3.5 (average pounds per carcass)
= 1.41 pounds of the carcass is breast quarters.

The breast quarters are 22.57 ounces, or 1.41 pounds of a 3.5-pound chicken carcass. This is the total weight for two portions. The EP and AS weight for one portion of a breast quarter is:

22.57 (total ounces of breast quarters) / 2 (portions per carcass)
= 11.285 ounces

*or*

1.41 (total pounds of breast quarters) / 2 (portions per carcass)
= .705 of a pound

If Johnny's EP and AS price for a whole chicken is $1.46 and the weight of one breast quarter is 11.285 ounces or .705 of a pound, the EP and AS price for one portion is

$1.46 (EP price per pound) / 16 (ounces per pound)
= $0.0913 per ounce

$0.0913 (price per ounce) × 11.285
= $1.03 (EP and AS cost for breast quarter)

*or*

$1.46 (EP price per pound) × .705 (of a pound)
= $1.03 (EP and AS cost for breast quarter)

If Johnny buys breast quarters at $1.89 per pound and serves an 11.285-ounce portion, or .705 of a pound, the EP or AS price for one portion is:

$1.89 (EP price per pound) / 16 (ounces per pound)
= $0.118 per ounce

$0.118 (price per ounce) × 11.285
= $1.33 (EP and AS cost for breast quarter)

*or*

$1.89 (EP price per pound) × .705 (of a pound)
= $1.33 (EP and AS cost for breast quarter)

Now Johnny is amazed. Originally, when he introduced his quarter-chicken special he divided the cost of a chicken carcass by 4 (or multiplied by 1/4, 25%, or .25) because he was able to serve four portions from one carcass. The per-portion cost was $0.87.

Now that the special has become popular and the breast quarter is outselling the leg quarter, a whole new cost scenario has presented itself. Johnny needs more breast quarters than leg quarters, so he is forced to do a cost comparison of buying the whole carcass or buying breast quarters. Johnny realizes that the actual cost of one breast-quarter portion from a whole carcass is $1.03. He then compares that to the actual cost of buying one breast-quarter portion of $1.33.

$1.33 (cost per portion for breast quarters)
− $1.03 (cost per portion for carcass) = $0.30

It cost $0.30 more per portion for Johnny to buy breast quarters than to cut a breast quarter from a whole carcass. The quandary is that Johnny needs more breast quarters than leg quarters. Should Johnny buy whole carcasses and stockpile leg quarters? Should Johnny's menu price for breast quarters reflect the higher product cost?

Johnny decided to do the same price comparison with the leg quarter. The leg quarters are 27.6 percent of the whole carcass. If a whole chicken weighs, on average, 3.5 pounds, then the leg quarters weigh:

56 ounces × .276 (leg quarters as a decimal)
= 15.46 ounces of thigh and leg quarter on a 3.5-pound carcass.

*or*

15.46 ounces / 16 (ounces in a pound) = .97 pound of leg quarters

*or*

.276 (thigh and leg quarter as a decimal)
× 3.5 (average pounds per carcass)
= .97 pound of the carcass is thigh and leg

The 15.46 ounces or the .97 pound represents the weight of two leg quarters. The EP and AS weight per portion is

15.46 (ounces for leg quarters) / 2 (portions per carcass)
= 7.73 ounces per portion

*or*

.97 (total pounds of leg quarters) / 2 (portions per carcass)
= .485 of a pound

If Johnny's EP and AS cost per pound is actually $1.46 and the leg quarter weighs 7.73 ounces or .485 of a pound, then the EP or AS cost per portion for a leg quarter is:

$1.46 (EP and AS cost per pound) / 16 (ounces per pound)
= $0.0913 cost per ounce

$0.0913 (cost per ounce) × 7.73
= $0.70 (EP and AS cost per leg quarter)

*or*

$1.46 (EP and AS cost per pound) × .485 (of a pound)
= $0.70 (EP and AS cost per leg quarter)

If Johnny buys leg quarters at $0.89 per pound and serves a 7.73-ounce portion or .485 of a pound, his EP and AS portion price is

$0.89 (price per pound) / 16 (ounces per pound)
= $0.056 price per ounce

$0.056 (price per ounce) × 7.73 (ounces per portion)
= $0.43 (EP and AS cost per leg quarter)

*or*

$0.89 (price per pound) × .485 (of a pound)
= $0.43 (EP and AS cost per leg quarter)

Again, the results of the cost comparison amaze Johnny. As mentioned earlier, he originally figured his quarter-chicken special portion cost cut from a whole carcass at $0.87. His leg quarter, from the whole carcass, has an actual EP and AS portion cost of $0.70. But what is truly amazing is that if Johnny buys leg quarters his EP and AS portion cost is only $0.43.

$0.70 (portion cost from carcass)
− $0.43 (cost per portion for leg quarters) = $0.27 cost savings

Johnny can save $0.27 per portion of leg quarters by purchasing them already portioned at $0.89 per pound. It costs Johnny $0.30 more per pound to buy breast quarters already portioned. Johnny now has to decide how to purchase for his half-chicken and quarter-chicken menu items.

Johnny decides to purchase whole chickens for his half-chicken menu items and to purchase breast quarters and leg quarters for his quarter-chicken menu items. Johnny's menu price for a breast quarter is higher than for a leg quarter. When his customers ask why, he explains that the portion size is larger and the cost for the breast quarter is $0.90 higher.

Anytime a chicken product is purchased, a price comparison should be performed. As you can see from Johnny G's example, the actual cost of a chicken portion is not always as it seems.

## Turkey, Ducks, and Geese

Turkeys are served on Thanksgiving, Christmas, New Year's Day, and Easter. Turkey is an inexpensive protein and can provide a profitable holiday for the food service operator. Whole turkeys are roasted and then carved and sliced for service. Turkey breasts are roasted and then sliced for service. When serving a whole turkey or a breast, the

$$\text{AP price per pound} < \text{EP and AS price per pound}$$

*and*

$$\text{AP weight} > \text{EP and AS weight}$$

Ducks and geese have the same AP to EP and AS relationships as a roasted turkey.

## Shellfish

Shellfish are animals that live in shells under water. They include both crustaceans and mollusks. The common crustaceans are crab, lobster, and shrimp. The common mollusks are clams, mussels, oysters, and scallops. All crustaceans and mollusks can be purchased fresh in their shells. Shrimp are available frozen in the shell or peeled and deveined. Other shellfish are removed from the shell before freezing, and all shellfish are removed from the shell before canning.

Fresh shellfish are priced by the each, by a certain number per pound, per bushel, or per gallon. Therefore, the portion cost for fresh shellfish is similar to buying any type of a portion-cut item.

The portion served is a set number of units—one lobster, four clams, eight scallops, and so on. The price per unit is easily determined. Since fresh shellfish are served by the unit,

$$\text{EP} = \text{AS}$$

*and*

$$\text{AP price per each} = \text{EP and AS price per each}$$

When fresh shellfish are purchased by the pound,

$$\text{AP weight} > \text{EP or AS weight}$$

because of moisture loss. The weight loss does create a yield variance, but it is not a consideration when determining a cost per portion because shellfish are served by the unit.

Shrimp scampi is served at Frank's Fresh Fish Fountain. Frank serves six extra jumbo shrimp per portion. Extra jumbo shrimp average 16 to 20 shrimp per pound with an AP price of \$9.95 per pound. What is the cost for the six shrimp Frank uses in one portion of scampi?

Extra jumbo shrimp average 16 to 20 each per pound. The average number of shrimp per pound is 18 shrimp:

$$16 \text{ shrimp} + 20 \text{ shrimp} = 36 \text{ shrimp}$$

$$36 \text{ shrimp} / 2 = 18 \text{ shrimp}$$

Therefore, if Frank serves 6 shrimp per portion and Frank averages 18 shrimp per pound, Frank can serve three portions of shrimp scampi using extra jumbo shrimp for every pound of shrimp he purchases.

18 (average number of shrimp per pound)
/ 6 (number of shrimp per portion) = 3 (portions per pound)

Frank pays \$9.95 per pound for extra jumbo shrimp. He averages 18 shrimp. What is the cost per shrimp?

\$9.95 (cost per pound) / 18 (average number of shrimp per pound)
= \$0.55 (cost per each shrimp)

What is the cost of the shrimp for one portion of shrimp scampi?

\$0.55 (cost per shrimp) × 6 (number of shrimp per portion)
= \$3.30 (cost for 6 shrimp)

*or*

$9.95 (cost for 18 shrimp) / 3 (number of portions per pound)
= $3.32 (cost per portion) (cost variance of $0.02 due to rounding)

Frozen shellfish are priced by the pound. Frozen shellfish still offers so many units of product per pound, but the effect of freezing and thawing can take a toll on the quality and usable count of a shellfish item. There is likely to be a more significant yield variance on a pound of frozen shellfish than on a pound of fresh (not old being sold as fresh) shellfish. Therefore, with frozen shellfish,

AP price per pound < EP or AS price per pound

*and*

AP weight > EP or AS weight

Frank had a problem purchasing fresh extra jumbo shrimp one day. Shrimp scampi is a static menu item, so Frank was forced to purchase the extra jumbo shrimp frozen. He purchased a 5-pound block of frozen 16 to 20 extra jumbo shrimp. As before, he expects an average 18 shrimp per pound. He set the frozen block in the refrigerator to thaw. When the block was defrosted, Frank looked at the shrimp.

Frank was disappointed with what he saw. He expected to have 90 usable extra jumbo shrimp for his scampi orders:

18 (shrimp per pound) × 5 (pounds) = 90 shrimp

He ended up with only 80. Ninety shrimp would have served 15 orders; 80 shrimp will only serve 13 orders.

90 (shrimp) / 6 (shrimp per order) = 15 orders

80 (shrimp) / 6 (shrimp per order)
= 13.33 orders (It is not possible to serve .33 or 1/3 of an order.)

So Frank decides to see what the yield is on the 5-pound block of frozen extra jumbo shrimp compared to 5 pounds of fresh shrimp.

80 (usable shrimp) / 90 (average per 5 pounds of fresh shrimp)
= 88.9% yield

Frank paid $8.00 per pound for the frozen shrimp. The total cost of the 5-pound block was

$8.00 (price per pound) × 5 (pounds)
= $40.00 (cost for 5 pounds frozen shrimp)

Frank's EP price per pound is

$8.00 (price per pound) / .889
= $9.00 (EP and AS price per pound)

The frozen shrimp cost

$8.00 (price per pound) / 16 (shrimp per pound)
= $0.50 (cost per shrimp)

One portion costs

$0.50 (cost per shrimp) × 6 (shrimp per portion) = $3.00

Frank realizes that even though his yield per pound is less with the frozen shrimp than the fresh shrimp, the price per pound is cheaper for the frozen product and, therefore, his portion cost is less.

## Finfish

Finfish are animals that live in fresh and salt water. Finfish can be flat or round. Some common varieties of finfish are cod, salmon, sole, and trout. Although federal grading of finfish is not mandatory, the grades for finfish are A, B, and C. Grade A is the highest grade and, therefore, the most expensive to purchase. Due to the fact that grading is not mandatory, the cost to purchase a graded finfish is higher per pound than a nongraded finfish.

Fresh finfish are highly perishable. The shelf life is one to two days. Therefore, it is critical that fresh finfish be purchased from a highly reputable supplier. As mentioned previously, sometimes buying frozen finfish is a much better alternative to buying fresh finfish. Some finfish sold as fresh have been previously frozen and then defrosted. Be careful when receiving this product.

Finfish has many market forms. They can be purchased whole or round. This is the fish as it was when taken out of the water. They can be purchased *drawn.* This form has the internal organs removed. A *dressed* finfish has its organs, scales, head, tail, and fins removed. Steaks are cut from a dressed finfish by slicing the finfish vertically, in 1-inch sections. A piece of the backbone is in each steak. Fillets are the boneless sides of the finfish. They can contain the skin or be skinless. Sticks are boneless slices cut from the fillet. Butterflied fillets are the finfish dressed and deboned.

Any market form of finfish can be purchased, or a whole or drawn finfish can be fabricated on-site. I would advise against purchasing a whole finfish unless your restaurant is next to the location

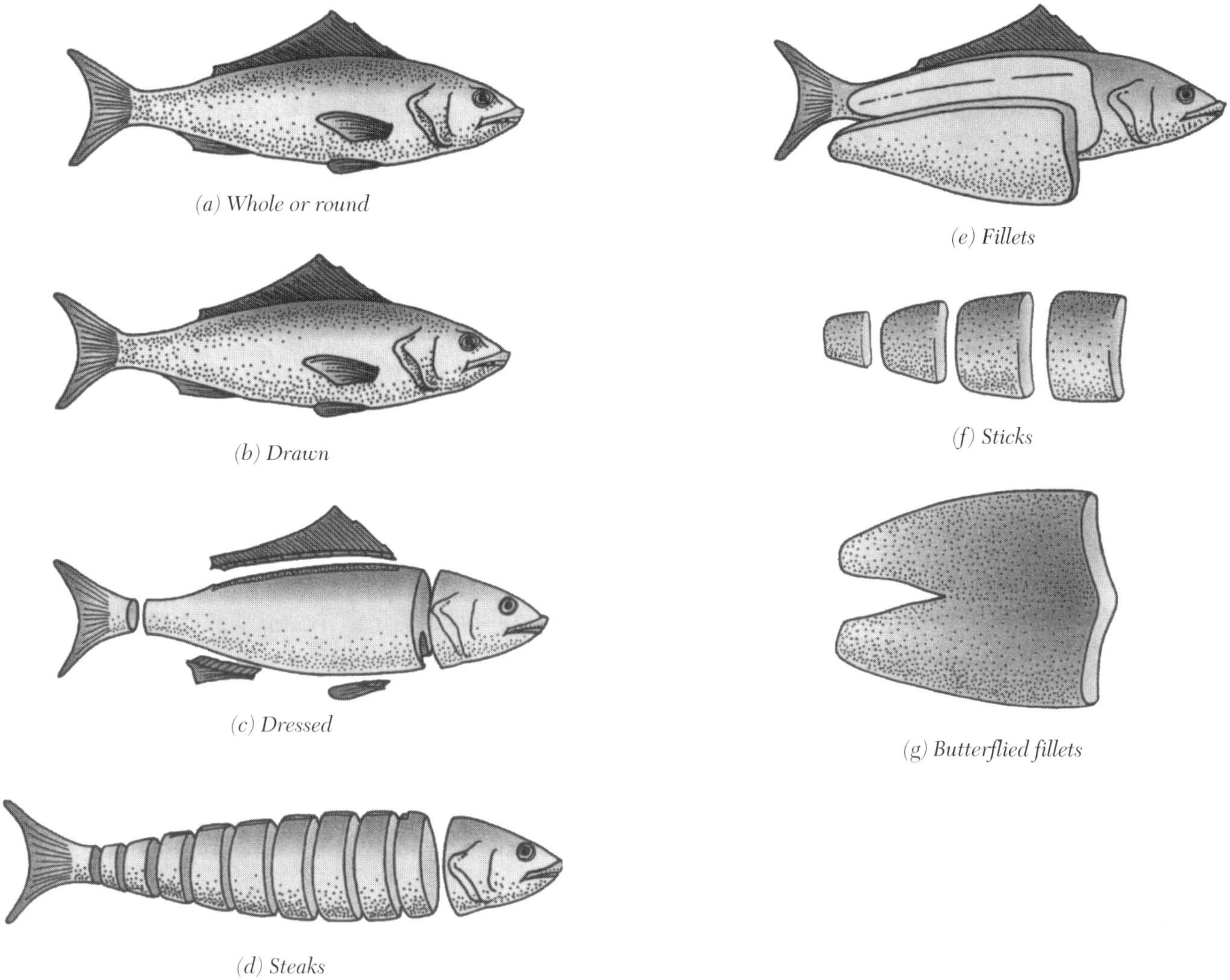


**FIGURE 4.3** The market forms of fish. (a) Whole or round fish. (b) Drawn. (c) Dressed. (d) Steaks. (e) Fillets. (f) Sticks. (g) Butterflied fillets. Courtesy *Professional Cooking,* Fifth Edition, by Wayne Gisslen, 2003: John Wiley & Sons, Inc., p. 361.

where the fish is caught. The internal organs should be removed as soon as possible after the fish is taken out of the water, or they can affect the quality of the product. All finfish purchased drawn and fabricated on-site will have a yield variance.

AP price per pound < EP and AS price per pound

*and*

AP weight > EP and AS weight

A drawn fish can be cooked and served, as is. This is common with a finfish like trout. In this scenario, the finfish is a portion-cut unit, therefore:

$$\text{AP price per each} = \text{EP and AS price per each}$$

and, due to the moisture loss that takes place during the cooking process,

$$\text{AP weight per each} > \text{EP or AS weight per each}$$

If the drawn finfish is fabricated on site, then the yield variance and its effect on price per pound needs to be considered. A flounder, purchased drawn, is priced at \$3.95 per pound. The yield on a flounder, drawn to fillet, is 45 percent. What is the price per pound for the fillet?

$$\$3.95 \text{ (AP price per pound) } / .45 = \$8.78 \text{ (EP and AS price per pound per fillet)}$$

The cost per pound for flounder fillet is 2.2 times that of the flounder drawn.

$$\$8.78 \text{ (EP and AS price per pound) } / \$3.95 \text{ (AP price per pound)} = 2.2 \text{ times}$$

You serve a 6-ounce flounder-fillet dinner. What is the cost per 6-ounce portion?

$$\$8.78 \text{ (EP and AS price per pound) } / 16 \text{ (ounces per pound)} = \$0.55 \text{ per ounce}$$

$$\$0.55 \text{ (price per ounce)} \times 6 \text{ (ounces per portion)} = \$3.30$$

Flounder, drawn, is purchased for \$3.95 per pound. The 6-ounce fillet cost from the flounder is \$3.30. In addition to the cost per portion, the cost of labor to fillet the flounder needs to be considered. Now that we know how expensive the portion cost is, there should be a comparison made between the cost of purchasing the flounder, drawn to the cost of purchasing flounder fillets. If the price of fillets is < or = to \$8.78, and the quality is equivalent, then the fillets should be purchased.

Center-of-the-plate items, other than chicken and turkey, are the most expensive items purchased in a food service operation. These items are the cornerstone of the menu. Understanding how these items change from their AP state to their EP and/or AS state ensures proper item costing and proper menu pricing.

## ACCOMPANIMENTS WITH A LOW FOOD COST

### Produce

Produce includes fruits and vegetables and it is used in every food service operation. The type and variety of produce available is seemingly endless. There are more than 8,000 varieties of apples alone. Produce consumption has increased dramatically in recent years as scientific research has proved some health benefits to eating produce.

Produce can be served in a variety of ways, limited only by your imagination. It can be an appetizer, a salad, an entree, a side dish, and even a dessert. Produce can be included in the menu price for an entree or priced a la carte. Produce is available in four market forms: fresh, frozen, canned, and dehydrated.

**Fresh Produce** Fresh produce is the most perishable form, and it must be refrigerated. The quality and price paid for fresh produce is directly related to the season of the year and the weather conditions. Under optimal growing conditions, the best quality and price is available in the United States during the spring and summer months. A large percentage of our fresh produce is imported during the fall and winter months.

Quality grades for fresh produce vary by type from U.S. No. 1, No. 2, or No. 3, to U.S. Extra Fancy or U.S. Fancy. It is not uncommon to purchase ungraded produce. Fresh produce is sold by the box, bunch, bushel, carton, crate, dozen, each, lug, pound, quart, or pint.

Some fresh items can be served AP, while others will need some trimming. The amount of trimming varies widely by the type of fresh product. The yield percentage for fresh produce can be anywhere from 100 percent for a potato served baked to under 50 percent for asparagus tips. Therefore, when costing a portion of fresh produce, if the item can be served AP, the yield percentage is equal to 100 percent. If the item must be trimmed, the yield percentage is < 100 percent. If the yield percentage is < 100 percent:

AP price per unit of measure
< EP and AS price per unit of measure

*and*

$$\text{AP unit of measure} > \text{EP and AS unit of measure}$$

Fresh strawberries can be served AP. If we purchase a quart of fresh strawberries and they are all edible,

$$\text{AP price} = \text{EP and AS price}$$

*and*

$$\text{AP unit of measure} = \text{EP and AS unit of measure}$$

If there is a certain percentage of fresh strawberries in the quart that are soft or moldy, or the strawberries are going to be sliced as a filling for a cake, and the stem portion discarded, then

$$\text{AP price} < \text{EP and AS price}$$

*and*

$$\text{AP unit of measure} > \text{EP and AS unit of measure}$$

The food service industry in the United States relies heavily on the abundance and availability of fresh produce. But we have absolutely no control over mother nature. A number of years ago, the entire winter fresh tomato crop from Florida was devastated by freezing temperatures. Prior to the Florida cold spell, a carton of fresh tomatoes was \$5.00. After the freeze, a carton of fresh tomatoes was \$50.00. That is a 900 percent increase in price:

$$\$5 + 5x = \$50$$

$$5x = 50 - 5 = 45$$

$$x = 45 \div 5 = 9$$

To get the percentage, move the decimal point two places—we multiply by 100 to do this:

$$9 \times 100 = 900\%$$

Every food service operation that used fresh tomatoes had to decide it they could afford to continue to purchase them or if they could eliminate them from their recipes. McDonald's Corp. decided they did not want to eliminate fresh tomato slices from their sandwiches, so they priced tomatoes on the international market. They found fresh tomatoes from Puerto Rico for $20.00 a carton. The price increase was only 300 percent.

Fresh produce is a valuable commodity to the food service industry. The wise operator uses the term *seasonal* on their menu items when they describe their fresh produce selections. That way, as the price of an item becomes too costly, another less expensive item can easily take its place.

**Frozen Produce** Frozen produce is commonly used when fresh produce is out of season. Vegetables freeze better than fruits. The quality of a frozen vegetable, in terms of color and texture, is much higher than that of frozen fruit. When fruit is frozen, it tends to discolor and to lose its texture.

Frozen vegetables can be served heated up, while frozen fruits are better used as a recipe-ready ingredient in cooking or baking. Frozen vegetables are available in units of 10 or 12 ounces, and 1, 2, 2.5, 3, or 5 pounds. Frozen fruits are available in units of 5, 10, or 12 ounces, and 1, 6, 6.5, 25, or 30 pounds.

The admirable quality of a frozen fruit or vegetable product is the yield. All of the trimming necessary to bring the product to its EP state is done before the product is frozen. Therefore, with frozen fruits and vegetable:

$$\text{EP} = \text{AS}$$

*and*

$$\text{AP price per unit} = \text{EP and AS price per unit}$$

*and*

$$\text{AP weight} = \text{EP and AS weight}$$

Frozen orange-juice concentrate is a frozen fruit product. When we reconstitute the orange juice, the can is thawed to a liquid state and water is added. The common ratio of water to liquid concentrate is 3:1. Therefore, the yield for frozen orange juice is greater than 100 percent. With this product:

$$\text{AP price per ounce} > \text{EP or AS price per ounce}$$

*and*

$$\text{AP volume} < \text{EP and AS volume}$$

If we purchase a 16-ounce can of frozen orange juice and we add three times that amount in water, the addition of three 16-ounce cans of water to 16 ounces of concentrate yields 64 ounces:

16 (oz. water) + 16 (oz. water) + 16 (oz. water)
+ 16 (oz. orange juice) = 64 ounces

The yield on this product is

64 ounces / 16 ounces = 4.00 or 400%

This is a 300 percent increase over the initial amount.

A 16-ounce can of orange-juice concentrate costs $1.60. One ounce costs $0.10.

$1.60 (cost for 16 ounces) / 16 = $0.10 per ounce

When the orange juice is reconstituted, it yields 64 ounces. The cost for the orange juice is still $1.60.

$1.60 (cost for 16 ounces) / 64 (ounce yield) = $0.025 per ounce

*or*

$0.10 (cost per ounce) / 4.00 (yield %) = $0.025 per ounce

The cost per ounce for EP and AS orange juice is actually $0.025.

**Canned Produce** Canned fruits and vegetables are very common, although every produce item is not available canned. The canning process causes discoloration and a texture change in vegetables. Fruits that are canned, like peaches, pears, and pineapple, seem to hold up well. Canned tomatoes are recipe-ready but could never be used sliced on a sandwich or in a salad.

The canning process necessitates the addition of liquid to the product inside of the can. When the can is opened, the liquid is drained. The "drained weight" is the actual product yield. The drained weight varies by type of product and can size. Common can sizes and their drain weight are listed in Table 4.1.

Produce is trimmed before the canning process. When the can is opened and the liquid is drained,

EP weight = AS weight

*and*

EP price = AS price

**TABLE 4.1**

Common Can and Jar Sizes (Average Net Weight or Fluid Measure and Average Volume Per Can)

| *Can Size* | *Average Net Weight or Fluid Measure per Can* | | *Average Volume per Can* | |
|---|---|---|---|---|
| | **Customary** | **Metric** | **Cups** | **Liters** |
| No. 10 | 6 lb (96 oz.) to 7 lb 5 oz. (117 oz.) | 2.72 kg to 3.31 kg | 12 cups to 13-2/3 cups | 2.84 L to 3.24 L |
| No. 3 Cyl | 51 oz. (3 lb 3 oz.) or 46 fl oz. (1 qt 14 fl oz.) | 1.44 kg or 1.36 L | 5-3/4 cups | 1.36 L |
| No. 2-1/2 | 26 oz. (1 lb 10 oz.) to 30 oz. (1 lb 14 oz.) | 737 g to 850 g | 3-1/2 cups | 0.83 L |
| No. 2 Cyl | 24 fl oz. | 709 mL | 3 cups | 0.71 L |
| No. 2 | 20 oz. (1 lb 4 oz.) or 18 fl oz. (1 pt 2 fl oz.) | 567 g or 532 mL | 2-1/2 cups | 0.59 L |
| No. 303 (old) | 16 oz. (1 lb) to 17 oz. (1 lb 1 oz.) | 453 g to 481 g | 2 cups | 0.47 L |
| No. 300 (new) | 14 oz. to 16 oz. (1 lb) | 396 g to 453 g | 1-3/4 cups | 0.41 L |
| No. 2 (Vacuum) | 12 oz. | 340 g | 1-1/2 cups | 0.36 L |
| No. 1 (Picnic) | 10-1/2 oz. to 12 oz. | 297 g to 340 g | 1-1/4 cups | 0.30 L |
| 8 oz. | 8 oz. | 226 g | 1 cup | 0.24 L |

*Source:* USDA Food and Nutrition Service, *Food Buying Guide for Child Nutrition Programs,* Revised November 2001, p. 1–30.

Due to the fact that the liquid is drained from the can before EP is obtained, when purchasing canned fruits and vegetables:

$$\text{AP weight} > \text{EP and AS weight}$$

*and*

$$\text{AP price per ounce} < \text{EP and AS price per ounce}$$

A No. 10 can of green peas weighs 6 pounds.

$$6 \text{ (pounds)} \times 16 \text{ (ounces in a pound)} = 96 \text{ ounces}$$

The drained weight of the green peas is 68 ounces.

$$68 \text{ (ounces)} / 16 \text{ (ounces in a pound)} = 4.25 \text{ pounds}$$

The yield for peas from a No. 10 can is

$$68 \text{ (ounces)} / 96 \text{ (ounces)} = .71 \text{ or a } 71\% \text{ yield}$$

*or*

4.25 (pounds) / 6 (pounds) = .71 or 71% yield

If you purchase a case of No. 10 cans of peas for $6.00, the cost per can is

$6.00 (cost per case) / 6 (cans per case) = $1.00 per can

If we serve a 3-ounce portion of canned green peas, we can serve:

68 (ounces) / 3 (ounce portion size)
= 22.67 servings (round to 22 servings)

If the cost per 22 servings is $1.00, then the cost per portion is

$1.00 (cost per can) / 22 (servings per can) = $0.0455 per portion

However, if we needed to have 6 EP and AS pounds of canned green peas, how many pounds AP would you need?

6 (pounds EP and AS) / .71 (yield %) = 8.45 pounds AP

If you needed 8.45 AP pounds of canned green peas, how many No. 10 cans would you need to open?

8.45 (AP pounds) / 6 (pounds per can) = 1.41 cans

You would need to open two No. 10 cans, and there would be some product left over.

Another scenario exists with canned produce. The yield on canned tomato paste, tomato puree, or crushed tomatoes is 100 percent. These canned items are used as ingredients in a recipe. Therefore, the cost per can times the number of cans used is added to the cost for all of the ingredients in the recipe. For example, crushed tomatoes are purchased in No. 10 cans. There are six No. 10 cans per case. A case cost $12.00. Each can costs

$12.00 (cost per case) / 6 (cans per case) = $2.00 (cost per can)

If we use two cans of crushed tomatoes in a tomato-sauce recipe, the cost for the crushed tomatoes is

$2.00 (cost per can) × 2 (number of cans used) = $4.00

The $4.00 is added to all of the other ingredients' cost to determine a cost for the entire recipe. Any time we used a canned product in a recipe, the cost for the entire can is added to the recipe cost.

**Dehydrated Produce** Produce is dehydrated by the removal of water from the product. This process can be accomplished by the addition of heat in a controlled environment or by the use of a chemical agent. Dried fruit is commonly used in its dehydrated form; therefore:

EP = AS

*and*

AP price = EP and AS price

*and*

AP weight = EP and AS weight

Mikayla's Magic Muffin Shop makes Cherry Muffins using dehydrated cherries in the muffin mix. Mikayla buys and uses the dehydrated cherries by the pound. If Mikayla pays $15.00 for a 5-pound bag of dried cherries, her per-pound cost is:

$15.00 (price per 5 pounds) / 5 (number of pounds)
= $3.00 per pound

If Mikayla uses 2 pounds of dried cherries per batch of muffins, the cost of the cherries in the recipe is

2 (pounds) × $ 3.00
= $6.00 (cost for dried cherries per batch of muffins)

Dried vegetables are reconstituted before cooking by the addition of water or stock. This process adds weight to the dried vegetables, therefore:

EP = AS

*and*

AP price > EP and AS price

*and*

AP weight < EP and AS weight

Susanna's Super Soup Shop is famous for its split pea soup. Susanna purchases and uses split peas by the pound. A pound costs $0.50. Before Susanna simmers her soup, she soaks her split peas in stock. Susanna begins the soaking process with 2 pounds of dried split peas but ends the process with 4.44 pounds of reconstituted split peas. What is the EP and AS cost for the 2 pounds of split peas?

$0.50 (AP cost per pound) × 2 (pound of peas)
= $1.00 (cost for 2 pounds dry peas)

But 2 pounds of dry beans turns into 4.44 pounds of reconstituted peas.

4.44 (pounds) / 2 (pounds) = 2.22 or a 222% yield

So the actual EP and AS cost per pound is less than (<) the AP cost per pound:

$1.00 (AP cost for 2 pounds) / 2.22 (yield as a decimal)
= $0.45 (EP and AS cost for 2 pounds)

## Dairy

Butter, hard and soft cheese, cream, frozen desserts, half and half, margarine, and milk are all dairy products. The dairy products used in the U.S. food service industry are from cow's milk. The fat content of cow's milk is from the cream. When the cows are milked, the cream rises to the top of the container. As the milk is pasturized and processed, the cream is either skimmed off or disbursed into the product. Skimming the cream off of the milk has two purposes. It creates a low-fat dairy product, and it allows for the production of items high in fat, like cream and butter.

The flavor and the texture of a dairy product depend on the percentage of cream in the product. Although cream is high in saturated fats, an item with a high fat content has a better taste and a higher price. Whole milk has the highest fat content and price of any milk product. Premium ice cream has the highest fat content and price of any ice-cream product.

Dairy products are widely used AP and as an ingredient in a recipe. Milk is used as a beverage and as an ingredient in a cream soup, sauce, or a baked item. A soft cheese can be used as a spread or sliced for an appetizer. Hard cheeses can be sliced for a sandwich or cubed for a buffet display. Cream can be used as an ingredient or whipped as a topping. Butter and margarine can be used as a spread or as an ingredient.

The best part about using dairy products, besides the flavor and texture they impart, is the yield. Dairy is the only food group without a yield variance, in theory anyway. If dairy items are used AP or are added to a recipe and they do not curdle, then

AP = EP and AS

*and*

AP price = EP and AS price

*and*

AP volume = EP and AS volume

*and*

AP weight = EP and AS weight

If the item does curdle due to excessive heat, then the entire recipe would need to be duplicated. Although this would double the actual cost to the operator, it is not because the yield of the dairy product had changed. It is because of human error.

At Dan's Dairy Delight, milk is purchased by the 5-gallon poly bag. The price for 5 gallons is $10.00. The price per gallon is

$10.00 (price for 5 gallons) / 5 (gallons per poly bag)
= $2.00 price per gallon

One quart costs

$2.00 (price per gallon) / 4 (quarts in a gallon) = $0.50 per quart

If Dan puts a quart of milk in his cream-soup recipe, the cost for the milk is $0.50.

The cost of milk per ounce is

$2.00 (gallon price) / 128 (ounces per gallon)
= $0.0156 cost per ounce

If Dan serves an 8-ounce glass of milk, the cost is

$0.0156 (cost per ounce) × 8 (ounces in one glass)
= $0.125 cost per portion of milk

Dan purchases cheese for $3.20 a pound. If Dan serves a 1-ounce slice of cheese on a sandwich, the slice costs

$3.20 (price per pound) / 16 (ounces in a pound)
= $0.20 per 1-ounce slice

The only dairy item that has a yield greater than 100 percent is whipping cream. Whipping the cream adds air and, therefore, volume to the product. However, whipping cream is purchased, measured, and priced by the AP fluid ounce.

If you purchase a quart of whipping cream, you have 32 ounces of product. After it is whipped, you will have 1/2 a gallon or 64 ounces of whipped cream. The yield percentage for whipping cream:

64 (ounces of whipped cream) / 32 (ounces of unwhipped cream) = 2.00, or 200%

## Pasta, Rice, and Legumes

Pasta is an unleavened dough made by combining flour with water and/or eggs. Then the dough is formed into any variety of different shapes and dried. Pasta is prepared by boiling. It can be purchased by the pound, or it can be made from scratch on site.

Rice is the edible seed of a semiaquatic grass. There are three classifications for rice based on the length of the seed: short grain, medium grain, and long grain. Rice is a common staple in a wide variety of cuisines. Rice is prepared by boiling and then simmering. It is purchased by the pound.

Legumes are the edible seeds of a plant that produces a single row of seeds inside of a pod. Some pods are also edible. Common legumes are black beans, kidney beans, pinto beans, and soya beans. Legumes are prepared by boiling and then simmering. They are purchased by the pound.

Pasta, rice, and legumes share a common method of preparation. They are all prepared by boiling and/or simmering in liquid. As they cook, they absorb moisture. The addition of moisture creates an uncommon yield percentage. All pasta, rice, and legumes have a yield percentage greater than 100 percent.

Ethnic cuisine is extremely popular today, and there are many restaurants that serve the cuisine of Mexico. Every entree is served with rice and beans. Let's see how cost-effective these side dishes are.

Pinto beans are purchased for $0.59 per pound. They are soaked in water and then boiled and simmered. The average portion size for pinto beans is 4 ounces. One pound of dry pinto beans yields 2.8 pounds cooked pinto beans. The yield percentage is:

2.8 (pounds cooked) / 1 (pound dry) = 2.80, or 280% yield

Dry pinto beans are $0.59 AP per pound, and the yield is 280 percent. The EP and AS price per pound is:

$0.59 (AP price per pound) / 2.80 (yield %)
= $0.21 EP and AS price per pound

An EP and AS pound of cooked pinto beans costs $0.21. One pound of cooked pinto beans will serve four 4-ounce portions.

16 (ounces in one pound) / 4 (ounces in one portion)
= 4 portions per pound

An ounce of cooked pinto beans costs

$0.21 (cost per EP and AS pound) / 16 (ounces per pound)
= $0.0131 cost per ounce

One portion of cooked pinto beans costs

$0.0131 (cost per ounce) × 4 (portion size in ounces)
= $0.0525 cost per portion

*or*

$0.21 (cost per EP and AS pound) / 4 (portions per pound)
= $0.0525 cost per portion

So the cost for the side of pinto beans served with your entree is just over $0.05.

White, medium-grain rice is purchased for $0.29 per pound. The rice is boiled and simmered in water. The average portion size for rice is 4 ounces. One pound of dry white, medium-grain rice yields 3 pounds of cooked rice. The yield percentage is

3 (pounds cooked) / 1 (pound dry) = 3.00, or 300% yield

White, medium-grain rice is $0.29 AP per pound, and the yield is 300 percent. The EP and AS price per pound is:

$0.29 (AP price per pound) / 3.00 (yield %)
= $0.0967 EP and AS price per pound

An EP and AS pound of cooked white, medium-grain rice costs $0.0967. One pound of cooked rice will serve four portions:

16 (ounces per pound) / 4 (ounces per portion)
= 4 portions per pound

An ounce of cooked rice costs

\$0.0967 (cost per EP and AS pound) / 16 (ounces per pound) = \$0.006 cost per ounce

One portion of cooked rice costs

\$0.006 (cost per ounce) × 4 (ounces per portion) = \$0.0240 cost per portion

*or*

\$0.0967 (cost per EP and AS pound) / 4 (portion per pound) = \$0.0242 cost per portion

The cost for the side of rice served with your entree is a little more than \$0.02 (rounding is responsible for slight difference in totals).

The side of pinto beans cost \$0.0525 and the side of rice costs \$0.0242. The total cost of the side dishes served with an entree is

| | |
|---|---|
| \$0.0525 | (pinto beans) |
| +\$0.0242 | (rice) |
| \$0.0767 | |

less than \$0.08. This is one reason a restaurant serving Mexican cuisine can be very profitable. The same holds true for a restaurant serving Italian cuisine if it has a lot of pasta dishes on the menu. Pasta, as previously noted, also had a yield of greater than 100 percent.

## Miscellaneous Items

There are many other items that we use daily in a food service operation. The majority of them are ingredients added to a recipe to produce a final product. Some of the items are costly, others are not.

**Fat and Oil** Fat and/or oil adds flavor and texture to any product and is a necessary ingredient in many recipes. The source of fat used in food service is from animals. Fat from beef, pork, chicken, and cows' milk is highly saturated. Saturated fat is considered a risk factor for heart disease and stroke. Fat is a solid at room temperature and is purchased by the pound. Examples of animal-fat products are butter, a milk-fat product, and lard, an animal-fat product.

Oil is from plants. Oil produced from corn, olive, or safflower plants, to name a few, is either a mono- or poly-unsaturated fat.

Mono- and poly-unsaturated fats are healthier for the heart than their saturated counterparts. Oil is a liquid at room temperature and is purchased by a volume unit of measure. There are many kinds of oils available today.

A variation of oil is a hydrogenated oil. A hydrogenated oil is a liquid that turns into a solid after it is processed. Hydrogenated oil products—like Crisco, Primex, and Sweetex—are used primarily in baking. Hydrogenated oil products are sold by the pound.

Fat and oil are not "served" to the guest on a plate. Fat and oil are ingredients used in recipes that are then served to the guest. The relationship between AP and EP and AS for fat is

AP price per pound = EP and AS price per pound

*and*

AP weight = EP and AS weight

and for oil:

AP price per volume unit of measure
= EP and AS price per volume unit of measure

*and*

AP volume = EP and AS volume

In Gerard's Garde Manger Kitchen, salad dressings are prepared for all of the outlets in the hotel. Many of the salad-dressing recipes use an oil or oil-based component, like mayonnaise. Oil is purchased in a volume unit of measure. One gallon, or 3.78 liters, is a common package size for oil. One gallon of oil costs $10.00. The basic recipe for mayonnaise calls for 3 quarts of oil. What is the cost for the oil that is used in the mayonnaise recipe?

$10.00 (cost per gallon) / 4 (quarts in 1 gallon)
= $2.50 (cost per quart)

$ 2.50 (cost per quart) × 3 (number of quarts in recipe)
= $7.50 recipe cost for oil

If you realize that 3 quarts is 3/4 or .75 of a gallon, you could figure it this way:

$$\frac{\$10.00}{1} \text{ (cost per gallon)} \times \frac{3}{4} \text{ (amount of the gallon needed)}$$
$$= 30 / 4 = \$7.50 \text{ recipe cost for oil}$$

*or*

$10.00 (cost per gallon) × .75 = $7.50 recipe cost for oil

If the recipe calls for 3 liters of oil, the costing of the oil is slightly different. The pack size is 3.78 liters for $10.00. There are several different ways that you can find the cost for 3 liters. We can determine a per-ounce cost for oil and multiply the cost per ounce by the number of ounces in 3 liters. There are 33.8 ounces in 1 liter.

$10.00 (cost of 1 gallon) / 128 (ounces in 1 gallon)
=$0.0781 cost per ounce

Then:

$0.0781 (cost per ounce) × 33.8 (ounces per liter)
= $2.64 cost of oil per liter

$2.64 (cost per liter) × 3 (liters in recipe)
= $7.92 recipe cost for 3 liters of oil

We can also determine the relationship of a gallon (128 ounces) to 3.78 liters by using ounces.

33.8 (ounces per liter) × 3 (liters used in recipe)
= 101.4 ounces in 3 liters

There are 101.4 ounces in 3 liters and 128 ounces in 1 gallon.

101.4 (ounces in 3 liters) / 128 (ounces in 1 gallon)
= .792 (3 liters are .792% of a gallon)

If 3 liters is .792 percent of a gallon, then 3 liters is .792 percent of the cost of a gallon.

$10.00 (cost per gallon) × .792 (3 liters as a % of a gallon)
= $7.92 recipe cost for 3 liters

Another option is to use a multiplier. The multiplier for the conversion of a quart to a liter is 1.0567. The cost per quart is $2.50 so the cost per liter is

$2.50 (cost per quart) × 1.0567 (multiplier for quart to liter)
= $2.64 cost per liter

Then:

$2.64 (cost per liter) × 3 (liters used in recipe)
= $7.92 recipe cost for oil

Brenda's Bake Shop produces the best cookies in town. The fat used in her cookie recipes is butter and/or shortening. These fats are solid at room temperature and are sold and used by weight. Primex, a shortening, costs $43.00 for a 50-pound case. If a cookie recipe calls for 1 pound of shortening, what is the cost for the shortening?

$43.00 (cost for 50 pounds) / 50 (pounds)
= $0.86 for 1 pound of shortening

One other area where we use a fat/oil product is in our deep-fat fryers. The product we use today is Mel Fry. Mel Fry is a liquid soy-oil product packed in a plastic container and overwrapped in a cardboard box. A case of Mel Fry weighs 35 pounds and costs $26.66. It takes 50 pounds of Mel Fry to fill one well of a standard-size deep-fat fryer. Most food service operations have a double fryer unit, which means we use 100 pounds of Mel Fry to fill the fryers.

How much does it cost to fill one fryer unit?

$26.66 (cost per 35 pounds) / 35 (pounds) = $0.762 per pound

$0.762 (cost per pound) × 50 (pounds to fill fryer)
= $38.1 to fill a standard-size fryer

What does it cost to fill a double unit?

$0.762 (cost per pound) × 100 (pounds to fill 2 units)
= $76.20 cost to fill a double fryer

*or*

$38.10 (cost to fill one unit) × 2 (2 units to fill) = $76.20

The other way to cost the oil to fill the fryer is by developing a multiplier that expresses the relationship of 50 pounds to 35 pounds.

50 (pounds to fill fryer) / 35 (pounds per case)
= 1.429 multiplier for 50/35

Then:

$26.66 (cost for 35 pounds) × 1.429 (multiplier)
= $38.09 cost for 50 pounds

The cost for the oil in the fryer is generally factored into the cost of a portion of french fries or other foods that are fried before serving.

**Flour and Sugar** Flour and sugar are used in any number of recipes, from roux to a flambé dessert. The greatest quantity of flour and sugar, however, is used for baking breads and desserts. Flour and sugar are purchased by the pound. In production baking, where exact measurements are critical to a successful product, flour and sugar are measured by the pound. Therefore, in baking:

AP price per pound = Ingredient cost per pound

*and*

AP weight = Ingredient weight

Bread flour costs \$20.00 for a 50-pound bag. If a recipe for bread uses 1 pound, 12 ounces of bread flour, what is the flour cost?

\$20.00 (cost per 50 pounds) / 50 (pounds)
= \$0.40 per pound of bread flour

There are 16 ounces in a pound, so 1 ounce costs

\$0.40 (cost per pound) / 16 (ounces per pound) = \$0.025 per ounce

12 (ounces) × \$0.025 (cost per ounce) = \$0.30 for 12 ounces

| | |
|---|---|
| 1 pound costs | \$0.40 |
| 12 ounces cost | <u>\$0.30</u> |
| Total cost for bread flour | \$0.70 |

If you realize that 12 ounces is 3/4 or .75 of a pound, you can multiply:

$$\frac{\$0.40}{1} \text{ (cost per pound)} \times 1\ 3/4 \text{ (amount of flour needed)}$$

$$\frac{\$0.40}{1} \times \frac{7}{4} = \frac{\$2.80}{4} = \frac{\$0.70}{1} = \$0.70$$

*or*

\$0.40 (cost per pound) × 1.75 (pounds used in recipe)
= \$0.70 cost for bread flour

**Herbs, Spices, and Seasonings** Herbs, spices, and seasonings are added to a recipe to add flavor and differentiate one product from another. Herbs can be purchased fresh or dried. Spices and seasonings can be purchased dried or as a liquid. These items are used in small quantities. The cost per recipe for herbs, spices, and seasonings is not significant. Generally, the cost for these items is added to the recipe cost as a percentage of the total cost.

A great variety of items can be use in a food service operation. Each item will create a different costing scenario with regard to AP and EP and/or AS price, weight or volume. The successful operator understands how these differing scenarios affect the actual cost of serving a plate of food.

## FOOD-PRODUCT GROUPS: REVIEW PROBLEMS

1. Which food groups have a yield variance between their AP state and their EP/AS state?

2. What factors or conditions create a yield variance between AP and EP?

3. What factors or conditions create a yield variance between EP and AS?

4. Which food-product group has a 100-percent yield?

5. Which food-product groups have a yield $>$ 100 percent ?

6. What effect does the food-product yield percentage have on EP/AS price?

7. For each of the items listed below:
   - What is the EP price per pound?
   - How many pounds should be purchased to serve 25 guests a 6-ounce portion?

   a. Beef item, AP price $2.29 per pound, 87-percent yield

   b. Turkey, AP price $0.59 per pound, 60-percent yield

   c. Finfish, AP price $3.99 per pound, 45-percent yield

8. For each of the items listed below:
   - What is the EP price per pound?
   - How many pounds should be purchased to serve 25 guests a 3-ounce portion?

   a. Fresh broccoli, whole, $0.99 per pound, 62.8-percent yield

b. Fresh carrots, whole jumbo, $0.59 per pound, 83.6-percent yield

c. Rice, white, medium-grain, $0.35 per pound, 303-percent yield

## Food-Product Groups: Review Answers

1. Any non-portion-controlled meat, poultry, finfish items; most fresh produce items, canned produce, cereal, grains, and rice

2. Peeling, trimming, cooking loss

3. Type of product, for example, a roast or a whole chicken; portion size, plate presentation

4. Dairy

5. Cereal, grains, and pasta

6. Items with a yield variance of less than 100 percent will have a higher EP/AS cost than AP cost.

   Items with a yield variance of greater than 100 percent will have a lower EP/AS cost than AP cost.

7. Formulas: $\frac{\text{AP price}}{\text{Yield \%}} = \text{EP price}$ $\frac{\text{AP weight}}{\text{Yield \%}} = \text{EP weight}$

   Total product needed: 25 6-ounce portions

   25 guests × 6 oz. = 150 oz. 150 oz. / 16 oz. = 9.375 pounds

   a. $2.29 / .87 = $ 2.63 EP price per pound, 9.375 lb. / .87 = 10.77 rounded to 11 pounds

   b. $0.59 / .60 = $0.98 EP price per pound, 9.375 lb. / .60 = 15.6 rounded to 16 pounds

   c. $3.99 / .45 = $8.87 EP price per pound, 9.375 lb. / .45 = 20.8 rounded to 21 pounds

**8.** Total product needed: 25 3-ounce portions

25 guests × 3 oz. = 75 oz. 75 oz. / 16 oz. = 4.69 pounds

a. $0.99 / $0.628 = $1.58 EP price per pound, 4.69 # / $0.628 = 7.47 rounded to 7.5, or 8 pounds

b. $0.59 / $0.836 = $0.71 EP price per pound, 4.69 lb. / $0.836 =
5.6 rounded to 6 pounds

c. $0.35 / 3.03 = $0.12 EP price per pound, 4.69 lb. / 3.03 = 1.55 rounded to 2 pounds

# Chapter 5
# INVENTORY MANAGEMENT

In a perfect world, we would receive daily deliveries of only the freshest ingredients in the exact quantities that we would use each day. Then we would not have any need for inventory. In the real world, where we try our hardest to estimate exactly how many covers we will serve and how much product we will use, and where products are delivered on a schedule that best suits the purveyor (unless we are an extremely large account), we must carry products in inventory.

## WHAT IS INVENTORY?

Food inventory is a current asset. Asset accounts are listed on the balance sheet. In order to be categorized as a current asset, an item must be purchased with the intent to sell and be converted into cash in less than one year. Perishable food inventory should be prepared and sold (converted into cash) in seven to ten days. Nonperishable items should not be held any longer than 30 days. Beverage inventory is different. Keg beer is best if consumed within two weeks of delivery. Canned and bottled beer should be consumed within six months of delivery. Distilled spirits can last indefinitely if properly stored. Then there is wine.

Wine, if properly stored, can be held in inventory for a long period of time. Some wine can actually appreciate in storage. *Appreciation* means the value of the wine increases, and it can be sold for substantially more than you paid for it. In a food service operation, we always sell the wine for a higher price than what we paid. A bottle of wine that appreciates has a much higher value that what we paid, and the reason is that the quality of the wine improves with age. If the wine has been purchased with the intention of selling it and is listed on the wine list, it is a current asset. If the wine has been purchased due to the potential for substantial appreciation and is not available for sale until it fully appreciates, it is a long-term asset.

## PURCHASING DIRECTS

Purchasing food and beverage products does not necessarily mean we are purchasing inventory. When products are ordered for use the day that they are delivered, these items are called *directs*. Directs go directly into production, and their cost is a part of the food cost for the day they are received.

Elaine's Elegant Elephant is having a special promotion on Friday evening. Elaine is offering a fresh Maine-lobster dinner with all the trimmings for $49.95. The special dinner is open to all of her customers, but reservations are required. There are 150 seats in the dining room. The deadline to make a reservation is on Tuesday.

Tuesday evening, Elaine reviews the number of reservations she has for the Friday evening lobster dinner. She has 138 reservations. On Wednesday morning, Elaine calls in her order for 138 fresh Maine lobsters to be delivered on Friday.

Friday afternoon, 138 fresh live Maine lobsters are delivered to Elaine's Elegant Elephant. They are checked to make sure they are indeed, still alive. Once the count of the live lobsters is complete, they are placed in the refrigerated walk-in, where they will stay until they are prepared for dinner that night.

The lobsters are $8.00 per pound and they average 1 1/2 pounds. The cost per lobster is

$8.00 (price per pound) × 1.5 (average weight per lobster) = $12.00

We purchased 138 lobsters at $12.00 per lobster:

138 (number of lobsters) × $12.00 (cost per lobster) = $1,656.00

The $1,656.00 that we paid for the lobsters is a direct food cost for Friday because the lobsters were received and sold on the same day.

## PURCHASING STORES (INVENTORY)

When we order food products in a quantity greater than can be used on the day they are delivered and received, we place the products into *inventory*. Inventory can be held in a dry storage area, a refrigerated storage area, or a frozen storage area. A well-run operation always has enough inventory on hand so the employees can prepare the menu items and the guests can be served.

### How Much Inventory Should We Purchase?

This is a critical question for a food service operation for several reasons. The first reason is the amount of secure storage space. Inventory has value and should be placed in a secure (locked) location. Therefore, we should not order more inventory than our available storage space. The second reason is the cost of the secure space. The cost of real estate and the square footage that is built upon it is expensive. These costs are necessary to run a food service operation. In addition to the dining room and kitchen, storage space must be allocated. But how much? Too little storage space creates the problems of not being able to secure inventory or possibly running out of products. Too much storage space creates the added cost of real estate, square footage, and heating and cooling the space. These costs vary greatly by location but must be considered, if possible, in the planning stages of the operation.

**FIGURE 5.1** Inventory in dry storage.
Photography by Thomas Myers.

The third reason is the issue of quality. As "fresh" or frozen foods age, the quality deteriorates.

If we order too much of a product that fits this category, the quality and the yield will decrease.

This will result in a higher than "planned" food cost and food-cost percentage.

The fourth reason is the actual cost of the inventory. When we purchase inventory, we need to pay for it shortly after it is received. That means that we must have the cash available to cover the cost of the items purchased for inventory. Inventory can be compared to a vault in a bank. The vault is where the money is stored. Inventory is where products are stored, but all of those products represent dollars. We paid money for those products. As we use our inventory, their cost is transferred from our inventory account (an asset account) to cost of food sold (a cost-of-sales account).

Today at Genny's Gourmet Catering Co., a Cornish-hen luncheon is being prepared to serve 60. The menu price per person for the Cornish-hen luncheon is $15.00. All of the food for the luncheon, including 60 Cornish hens, has been taken out of inventory early this morning. The total cost of food taken from inventory is $150.00. The total revenue from the luncheon is $900.00.

$15.00 (menu price) × 60 (number of guests)
= $900.00 total revenue

The total cost of food sold (the cost of items removed from inventory) is $150.00. The gross profit is $750.00.

| | |
|---|---|
| Revenue | $900.00 |
| Cost of food sold | $150.00 |
| Gross Profit | $750.00 |

The food cost percentage is 16.67 percent:

$150.00 (cost of food) / $900.00 (selling price) = .1667, or 16.67%

The cost of food taken out of inventory this morning at Genny's Gourmet Catering Co. becomes the cost of food sold for the luncheon that Genny and Co. catered today.

## Inventory Valuation and Quantity

The dollar value and quantity of items in inventory must be accurately accounted for. This process uses basic mathematical applications following a simple pattern. The importance of accurately valuing inventory is truly critical to a successful food service operation. Accurate valuation tells us if we have enough product in stock or if we need to place an order, it tell us how much money we have in inventory (our vault), and it gives us the current information that we need to prepare our financial statements.

There are two methods that are used to keep track of the quantity and value of products in inventory. The two methods really work together and create a system of checks and balances. The methods are called *perpetual inventory* and *periodic inventory*.

## Perpetual Inventory

A perpetual inventory is a running list of products in inventory and their value. A perpetual inventory works like this:

Russell's Restaurant has a large area for dry storage inventory. When products are received at the dock, if they are canned, bottled (glass or plastic), in bags, or in cardboard boxes, they are brought to the dry storage area. Let's use 50-pound bags of sugar for our example.

There are three 50-pound bags of sugar in dry storage. The bags cost $25.00 each. A perpetual inventory form in the office lists this information. Two 50-pound bags of sugar are received today. The two bags are moved to the dry storage area and placed on the shelf where sugar is stored. In order to maintain a perpetual inventory, the two new bags of sugar are added to the form, and now there are a total of five 50-pound bags of sugar in inventory.

Later that day, when the baking crew arrives, one 50-pound bag of sugar is requisitioned from dry storage. Now the form is adjusted again, but this time one bag is subtracted from the form. Now the form says that there are four 50-pound bags of sugar in inventory.

*Perpetual Inventory Form*
*Sugar, 50# bag*

| *Date* | *Quantity* | *Value* |
|---|---|---|
| June 3, 20XX | 3 | $ 75.00 |
| June 7, 20XX | 5 | $125.00 |
| June 7, 20XX | 4 | $100.00 |

As new items are received and physically added to inventory, they are also added to the perpetual inventory form. As products are requisitioned from inventory and placed into production, the items are subtracted from the perpetual inventory form. The perpetual inventory forms are updated every time there is a change in the number and/or value of items in inventory. This way, we always have a correct count and value of our inventory. At least this is how it works in theory.

However, there could be a mistake on the perpetual inventory form, for a variety of reasons. An employee may have made a simple mistake and placed an item in the wrong location and then it was added to the wrong form. An employee may have taken the wrong item out of inventory and then the count of the wrong item and the right item would be incorrect. How do we check our perpetual inventory numbers to ensure that they are accurate? We ensure the accuracy of our perpetual inventory by conducting a physical inventory.

## Physical Inventory

A physical inventory is conducted by sending two employees into the storage areas to count all of the items on every shelf. Two employees are used for internal control and for speed. One employee counts the products on each shelf while the other employee writes down the count. The physical inventory is then compared to the perpetual inventory to ensure accuracy.

Let's return to the 50-pound bags of sugar. The last count we had on our form was four bags. For this example, let's say that, instead of the bake shop receiving a 50-pound bag of sugar, they received a 50-pound bag of flour. The sugar form says there are only four bags of sugar in inventory, but the physical inventory shows there are five bags of sugar. The count on the 50-pound bags of flour is incorrect as well. There is one less bag of flour in inventory than the perpetual inventory form shows. In this example, it is easy to determine that the flour instead of the sugar was given to the bake shop. It was a simple error. Now both the sugar and flour perpetual inventory forms need to be adjusted to equal the count from the physical inventory.

As the physical inventory "count" is compared to the perpetual inventory "count," any discrepancies, like the sugar and flour example, need to be investigated. It is important that we at least attempt to find out why there is a difference between what we should have (perpetual) and what we actually have (physical). Adjustments will need to be made to the perpetual inventory counts to equal the physical inventory counts.

Inventory storage areas are a vault where we keep our money. If product is missing, it is possible that someone is stealing our products or using them incorrectly. If this is the case, we need to figure this out as soon as it is noticed because every dollar we "lose" in inventory value is a dollar we lose in profit.

## Monthly Inventory Calculations

Food service operations prepare monthly financial statements. Accurate inventory value and usage in dollars is needed to prepare these statements. The physical inventory is counted at the close of business on the last day of the month. This way we have accurate information with which to prepare our month-end financial statements.

Inventory values and usage are determined for our financial statements using the following standard formula:

Beginning inventory (BI) (Close of inventory from last month)

+ Purchases (all inventory purchases for the month)

Cost of food available for sale

− Ending inventory (EI) (from the comparison of the physical to the perpetual)

Cost of food sold for the month

If we are preparing our month-end financial reports for the month of July 20XX, our beginning inventory value is the ending inventory value from the month of June 20XX. The other information that we need in order to arrive at a cost of food sold is the total value of all of our food purchases that went into inventory during the month and the current, adjusted, ending inventory for July 20XX.

If our ending inventory value for June 20XX was $3,700.00, and we purchased $14,400.00 worth of products that were placed into inventory, and our month-end inventory value is $4,500.00, what is our cost of food sold for the month of July 20XX?

| | |
|---|---|
| BI | $ 3,700.00 |
| + Purchases | 14,400.00 |
| Goods available for sale | $18,100.00 |
| − EI | 4,500.00 |
| Cost of Food Sold | $13,600.00 |

For the month of July 20XX, our cost of food sold is $13,600.00. If our food-sales revenue for July 20XX is $54,400.00, what is our food-cost percentage for July 20XX?

$$\frac{\text{Cost of food sold}}{\text{Food sales revenue}} = \text{Food cost percentage}$$

$$\frac{\$13{,}600.00}{\$54{,}400.00} = .25\text{, or } 25\%$$

Remember that our food cost is a part or a portion of our food-sales revenue. A part or a portion of a number yields a decimal or a percentage. If we cannot determine an accurate value for our inventory, then our financial statements as well as our food-cost percentage will not be correct. If our inventory information is inaccurate, then we cannot determine if we are really making any profit.

## INVENTORY TURNOVER RATE

How can we evaluate whether we are purchasing and maintaining the correct amount of products in inventory? The answer is simple. There is a mathematical formula that gives us this information. The mathematical formula is known as the *inventory turnover rate*. The formula is a two-step process. Step 1 is to determine the average value of products in inventory for a month.

**STEP 1:**

$$\text{Average food inventory for the month} = \frac{\text{Beginning inventory} + \text{Ending inventory}}{2}$$

Step 2 is to divide the cost of food used in the month by the average inventory for the month.

**STEP 2:**

$$\text{Food inventory turnover rate} = \frac{\text{Cost of food used for the month}}{\text{Average food inventory for the month}}$$

Using the beginning and ending inventory values from the month of July 20XX, the beginning inventory is $3,700.00 and the ending inventory is $4,500.00. Compute the average inventory for the month of July 20XX:

**STEP 1:**

$$\text{Average inventory for the month} = \frac{\$3{,}700.00 + \$4{,}500.00}{2}$$

$$= \frac{\$8{,}200.00}{2} = \$4{,}100.00$$

The cost of food used in July 20XX was $13,600.00.

**STEP 2:**

$$\text{Food inventory turnover} = \frac{\$13{,}600.00}{\$4{,}100.00}$$

$$= 3.3171, \text{ rounded to } 3.32$$

The inventory turnover rate of 3.32 means that the inventory was used and replaced 3.32 times during the month of July 20XX. An average month has 30 days, so if you turn your inventory 3.32 times, you are basically turning your inventory once every nine days. This is a healthy turnover rate for a food service operation.

30 (days per month) / 3.32 (turnover rate) = 9 days

The inventory turnover rate helps to clarify two points for the food service operator. The first point is that we do not want to tie up more money than necessary in inventory. If our turnover rate is in the range of three to four turns per month, then we are selling the products in inventory every 8 to 10 days.

30 (days per month) / 3 (as a turnover rate) = 10 days

30 (days per month) / 4 (as a turnover rate) = 7.5 days

Therefore, we are collecting sales revenue from our investment in food products three to four times per month. This range tells us we are not overbuying inventory items or tying up too much money in inventory.

This range also tells us that our products are not deteriorating in quality because they are being used in a timely manner. Remember, fresh and frozen products will deteriorate and their yield will shrink the longer they are kept in storage. A turnover rate in the range of three to four times per month means that products are being received and then sold to our customers on a regular basis.

Inventory management is important for meeting financial goals, for preparing financial statements, and for insuring food-product quality.

## Inventory Management: Review Problems

1. Why is inventory management so important for a food service operation?

2. Which financial statement contains the month-end inventory value?

3. What is the formula for determining the month-end cost of sale?

4. What is a perpetual inventory?

5. What is a physical inventory?

6. What is the name given to the value of the inventory products used during the month?

7. Which financial statement would require the information from question 6?

8. What additional information, besides inventory usage, would we need to complete our month-end financial statements?

**Monthly Inventory Calculations**

| For the month of October 20XX: | For the month of November 20XX: |
|---|---|
| Beginning Inventory: $ 5,400.00 | Beginning Inventory: $ ? |
| Purchases: $15,250.00 | Purchases: $ 18,500.00 |
| Ending Inventory: $ 4,800.00 | Ending Inventory: $ 5,200.00 |

9. What is the dollar value of goods available for sale in October?

10. What is the cost of food sold in October?

**11.** If October's sales revenue is $50,000.00, what is the food-cost percentage?

**12.** What is our beginning inventory for November 20XX?

**13.** What is the dollar value of goods available for sale in November?

**14.** What is the cost of food sold in November?

**15.** If November's sales revenue is $60,000, what is the food-cost percentage?

**16.** What is the inventory turnover rate for October and November?

## Inventory Management: Review Answers

**1.** It affects cash flow. If inventory quantities are larger than they need to be, we are tying up too much money. It also affects product quality and yield.

**2.** The balance sheet

**3.** BI + purchases = Cost of goods available − EI = Cost of food sold

**4.** Perpetual inventory is a list of every item and its value that should be in inventory.

**5.** Physical inventory is a count of every item actually in inventory.

**6.** Cost of goods (food) sold

**7.** The income statement or profit and loss statement

**8.** The value of directs

### Monthly Inventory Calculations

**9.** $20,650.00

10. \$15,850.00
11. 31.7 percent
12. \$4,800.00
13. \$23,300.00
14. \$18,100.00
15. 30.2 percent
16. October: Avg Inv = \$5,100; TO = 3.1
    November: Avg Inv = \$5,000; TO = 3.6

# Chapter 6

# PRODUCTION PLANNING AND CONTROL

The actual pre-prep and final preparation of food in an operation needs to be organized and well planned in order for the business to be successful. The planning process includes developing production forecasts and ensuring all resources needed to fulfill the forecast are available. Accurate forecasting can be a difficult task but there is information available to help us to achieve this goal.

## PRODUCTION FORECASTS

A production forecast begins with an educated estimate of the number of customers that will visit your restaurant and the menu items they will select during a specific meal period. This is incredibly difficult in a new food service operation but not in an established restaurant with the same or a similar menu. There, it is a matter of mathematically applying current information to the sales history. Computer technology is extremely beneficial in forecasting, but forecasting was done before the technology was available.

An accurate sales history contains the following information: the day of the week, the weather forecast and the actual conditions, the activities that are taking place within a certain radius of the operation or inside of the hotel, and the actual customer counts and sales per item.

A well-run operation has a date book at the hostess station. The date book specifies the day of the week, for example, Sunday, July 6. The hostess can add additional information that is valuable for forecasting business in the future. Information such as the fact that this was a three-day weekend. (The Fourth of July must have been Friday if Sunday is July 6.) This is not a "normal" Sunday because of the holiday on Friday. This information is written in the date book.

Weather and the seasons of the year are factors that affect business in a restaurant. If the weather is beautiful and it is summer, many of your customers may opt to have a barbeque, or they might be on vacation. If you are located in a tourist destination, a three-day weekend in summer will boost your customer counts. If it is raining, customers may get cabin fever and opt to eat out. In the winter when the snow is falling and the news is advising people to stay indoors, the road conditions will affect your customer counts. This information is written in the date book.

If there is a weekend craft show close to your restaurant, it will impact your business. Room sales affect restaurant sales in a full-service hotel. A convention inside of the hotel will impact hotel restaurant sales. If the attendees have all of their meals included in the convention package, it will decrease restaurant sales. If meals are only partially included for the attendees, it will increase restaurant sales for certain meal periods. Local events, hotel occupancy rates, and convention group information is written in the date book.

All of the information contained in the date book is utilized along with the sales history for that day. The sales history is a breakdown of the number of customers served each day, by meal period and by item(s) ordered. It is obtained by pressing the appropriate key on the point-of-sale (POS) computer terminal or by manually going through guest checks. The sales history is the crucial piece of information needed to develop an accurate production forecast. Let's examine the procedure for developing a production forecast. It begins with the menu. Sammy's by the Seaside is a popular dinner house. The dinner menu offers six entree items.

**DINNER MENU**

ENTREES

1
Beef Stew with Assorted Vegetables
$12.95

2
Roast Prime Rib of Beef, Au Jus
$18.95

3
Chicken a La Sammy
$15.95

4
Catch of the Day
$ Market Price

5
Shrimp Kabob with Wild Rice
$21.95

6
Sammy's Surprise
$19.95

It is Sunday, July 6, at 11:30 P.M., and Sammy is closing for the day. Sammy hits the appropriate key on the POS system and the following information prints out:

*Total number of customers:* *350*

| | *Total Items Sold:* | *Percentage:* |
|---|---|---|
| Entree 1: | 25 | 7.1% |
| Entree 2: | 120 | 34.3% |
| Entree 3: | 65 | 18.6% |
| Entree 4: | 35 | 10.0% |
| Entree 5: | 90 | 25.7% |
| Entree 6: | 15 | 4.3% |
| Total Sold: | 350 | 100% |

How did the POS system come up with the percentage of customers that ordered each item? Simply by dividing the number of each entree sold by the total number of entrees sold.

Entree 1: $\dfrac{25 \text{ (entrees sold)}}{350 \text{ (total sold)}}$ = .0714, or 7.14% of entrees sold is entree 1

Entree 2: $\dfrac{120 \text{ (entrees sold)}}{350 \text{ (total sold)}}$ = .3429, or 34.29% of entrees sold is entree 2

Entree 3: $\dfrac{65 \text{ (entrees sold)}}{350 \text{ (total sold)}}$ = .1857, or 18.57% of entrees sold is entree 3

Entree 4: $\dfrac{35 \text{ (entrees sold)}}{350 \text{ (total sold)}}$ = .10, or 10.00% of entrees sold is entree 4

Entree 5: $\dfrac{90 \text{ (entrees sold)}}{350 \text{ (total sold)}}$ = .2571, or 25.71% of entrees sold is entree 5

Entree 6: $\dfrac{15 \text{ (entrees sold)}}{350 \text{ (total sold)}}$ = .0429, or 4.29% of entrees sold is entree 6

Total: 1.00, or 100%

This information tells us what percentage of guests on Sunday, July 6, ordered each entree item. This information, by itself, is not a valid predictor of future Sunday sales. However, this information, along with Sunday sales from past weeks, past three-day weekends, and last year will give us valid information to forecast future Sunday sales. Accurately forecasting future Sunday sales ensures that the restaurant will have adequate supplies of necessary resources to serve the guests. Resources critical to serving guests are food and labor.

Sammy examines the sales information from July 6, and begins to think about next Sunday, July 13. He begins the forecasting process by estimating the number of customers that will come to dinner next Sunday. He starts by checking the customer counts from last year's equivalent date and the past five weeks of sales history.

July 12 is the date of the equivalent Sunday from last year.

| | |
|---|---|
| July 12: last year's dinner customer count | 185 |
| June 8: five weeks ago dinner customer count | 205 |
| June 15: four weeks ago dinner customer count | 235 |
| June 22: three weeks ago dinner customer count | 215 |
| June 29: two weeks ago dinner customer count | 225 |
| July 6: one week ago (three-day weekend) | 350 |

By reviewing the sales figures for last year and the past five weeks, Sammy determines that Sunday sales are slightly higher than they were one year ago, and a three-day weekend increases the number of customers that come to dinner on Sunday. Sammy decided the most accurate forecast of next Sunday's customer count will be an average of the four Sundays from June 8 to June 29.

Therefore, Sammy adds the customer counts from the aforementioned Sundays and divides by 4.

205 (June 8) + 235 (June 15) + 215 (June 22) + 225 (June 29) = 880

then:

880 (total dinner customers for a 4-week period) / 4 = 220

The forecast for the number of customers we will serve for dinner on Sunday, July 13, is 220.

Sammy now has the forecast of the number of customers that will come to dinner on Sunday, July 13. Next, Sammy will forecast the expected number of sales of each entree. To do this he reviews the percentage of each item purchased by his customers over the past five Sundays and the equivalent Sunday from last year. To expedite this process, for this example, Sammy will only forecast sales for entree 1.

Entree 1 sales by number and percentage (%) for last year and the past five weeks:

July 12: 12 (entrees sold) / 185 (total customers) = .0649 or 6.49%

June 8: 15 (entrees sold) / 205 (total customers) = .0732 or 7.32%

June 15: 20 (entrees sold) / 235 (total customers) = .0851 or 8.51%

June 22: 10 (entrees sold) / 215 (total customers) = .0465 or 4.65%

June 29: 25 (entrees sold) / 225 (total customers) = .1111, or 11.11%

July 6: 25 (entrees sold) / 350 (total customers) = .0714, or 7.14%

Now Sammy calculates the average number of customers that order entree 1. (Sammy uses the six weeks of sales history because it increases the validity of the average.) The average can be determined in one of two ways. Sammy can add the total number of entree 1 sold and divide by the total number of customers for the aforementioned weeks:

12 + 15 + 20 + 10 + 25 + 25
= 107 (total number of entree 1 sold)

185 + 205 + 235 + 215 +225 + 350
= 1,415 (total number of customers served)

Then:

107 (total number of entree 1 sold)
/ 1,415 (total number of customers served) = .0756, or 7.56%

Or he can add the six percentages and divide by 6.

.0649 + .0732 + .0851 + .0465 + .1111 + .0714
= .4522 (total sales represented as a decimal)

Then:

.4522 (total sales represented as a decimal) / 6 = .0754, or 7.54%
(rounding accounts for slightly different totals)

The average percentage of total guests who ordered entree 1 for the six Sundays analyzed is .075, or 7.5 percent. If Sammy forecasts 220 customers for Sunday, July 13, and .075, or 7.5 percent order entree 1, how many would be expected to order entree 1?

220 (forecasted customer count)
× 7.5% (percentage of entree 1) = 16.5, rounded to 17

Entree 1 sales forecast for Sunday, July 13, is 17 covers.

Sammy would continue to develop average sales percentages for entrees 2 thru 6 and multiply the average percentage sold by the forecasted 220 customer count. Then he would estimate how many pounds of stew beef, chicken, catch of the day, shrimp, vegetables and rice, prime rib roast, and surprise ingredients to purchase and prepare for Sunday, July 13. How does Sammy know how much food to purchase to serve 220 customers on Sunday, July 13? He knows how much food to purchase because he uses standardized recipes and standardized portion sizes.

## STANDARDIZED RECIPES

A *standardized recipe* is a list of ingredients and their exact unit of measure, along with complete preparation instructions. By using a standardized recipe we produce a consistent product with a consistent yield and a consistent portion size. The cost to prepare a standardized recipe should be within a certain range, depending on the ingredients and how they fluctuate in the marketplace. If this is indeed the case, we can determine a fair and profitable menu price based on the items' portion cost.

A standardized recipe is written in a standardized format. The format looks similar to this:

**Standardized Recipe Format**

| | | |
|---|---|---|
| Name: | | Yield: |
| Preparation and Cooking Time: | | Number of Portions: |
| | | Portion Size: |
| Quantity | Ingredients | Preparation Method |

### Quantity

Quantities are given in the most accurate unit of measure available. Weight, such as pounds, ounces, kilograms or grams, should be used for items that are commonly measured and purchased by weight. Meats, poultry, finfish, and certain fruits and vegetables are examples of items measured and purchased by weight. Volume is the best unit of measure for items that are liquid at room temperature. These items are purchased and priced by a volume unit of measure. Volume units of measure include gallon, quart, pint, cup, fluid ounce, tablespoon, teaspoon, liter, and milliliter. A measuring cup or spoon is necessary to accurately measure volume. Juice, milk, and oil are examples of products that are measured and purchased in volume units.

Count is the least accurate unit of measure used in a standardized recipe. Count means we use so many "each" of an item. Count is used when the "each" are fairly consistent or when we portion and serve by the each. Eggs and shellfish are examples of items that are measured and possibly purchased by count.

### Ingredients

Ingredients are listed in order of use and can be described as AP, EP, or recipe ready. If the preparation of a recipe calls for items to be sautéed, then a fat/oil product would be the first item on the list. If we are preparing beef stew, the description for the beef could read "beef, round", or "beef, 1-inch cubes."

## Preparation Method

This column describes how the quantities and ingredients are introduced and joined together to develop the final presentation. The descriptions use color, texture, and aroma to explain how the ingredients should "look and feel" before going on to the next step in the recipe. Remember, the most accurate measurements and the finest ingredients will not produce a wonderful meal if the preparation is incorrect.

## Recipe Yield and Conversion

A standardized recipe that is followed correctly will produce a specific yield and number of portions. The yield can be described by weight, volume, pan size, and/or number of portions. For example, an AP 20-pound roast will yield an EP 15-pound roast or thirty 8-ounce portions. A recipe for cream of broccoli soup will yield two gallons, or thirty-two 8-fluid-ounce portions. A recipe for lasagna will yield four 200 pans and, when cut 4 × 6, will yield 96 portions. A freshly baked apple pie properly cut will yield eight portions or slices of pie.

**FIGURE 6.1** A production kitchen.
Photography by Thomas Myers.

Look at this standardized recipe from Sammy's dinner menu for Beef Stew with Assorted Vegetables.

**Beef Stew with Assorted Vegetables**

Preparation and Cooking Time: 3.5 hours    Yield: 2 quarts
Portion Size: 8 fluid ounces    Number of Portions: 8

| *Quantity* | *Ingredients* | *Preparation Method* |
|---|---|---|
| 4 lbs. | Beef chuck, cubed | This is not a "real" recipe. |
| 1 lb. | Onion, diced | |
| 2 lbs. | Baby carrots | Do not prepare. |
| 1 lb. | Celery, sliced | |
| 1 lb. | Green peas | (For text example only) |
| 2 qts. | Beef stock | |

This recipe yields eight portions. The forecast for entree 1, Beef Stew with Assorted Vegetables, for Sunday, July 13, is 17 orders. How can we serve 17 orders if the recipe serves only 8? We can increase or decrease the yield of the recipe by determining the "correct" number to multiply all of the ingredients by. The number is a multiplier and/or a *conversion factor*. The process is simple. Recall the formula from Chapter 1:

$$\frac{\text{New yield}}{\text{Old yield}} = \text{Multiplier or conversion factor}$$

Sammy's new yield is 17 and his old yield is 8; therefore, the multiplier is

$$17 \text{ (new yield)} / 8 \text{ (old yield)} = 2.125$$

Or, Sammy could take the total number or ounces for the new yield divided by the total number of ounces for the old yield:

$$\frac{\text{New yield} = 17 \times 8 \text{ (ounce portions)}}{\text{Old yield} = 8 \times 8 \text{ (ounce portions)}} = \frac{136 \text{ ounces}}{64 \text{ ounces}} = 2.125$$

Then, Sammy will multiply all of the ingredient quantities by 2.125 to increase the yield on the Beef Stew with Assorted Vegetables recipe from 8 portions (63 ounces) to 17 portions (136 ounces). Now look at the standardized recipe.

**Beef Stew with Assorted Vegetables**

Preparation and Cooking Time: 3.5 hours

Yield: 2 qts. × 2.125 = 4.25 qts.

Portion Size: 8 fluid ounces

Number of Portions: 17

| *Quantity* | *Ingredients* |
|---|---|
| 4 lbs. × 2.125 = 8.5 lbs. | Beef chuck, cubed |
| 1 lb. × 2.125 = 2.125 lbs. | Onion, diced |
| 2 lbs. × 2.125 = 4.25 lbs. | Baby carrots |
| 1 lb. × 2.125 = 2.125 lbs. | Celery, sliced |
| 1 lb. × 2.125 = 2.125 lbs. | Green peas |
| 2 qts. × 2.125 = 4.25 lbs. | Beef stock |

(.125 lb. = 2 ounces, 4.25 quarts = 1 gallon, 1 cup)

*Preparation Method*

This is not a "real" recipe.

Do not prepare.

(For text example only)

Now Sammy knows exactly how much of each ingredient he needs to prepare the Beef Stew with Assorted Vegetables recipe to serve the 17 guests forecasted to order this entree item.

## Recipe Cost and Portion Cost

Now that Sammy has the revised quantity of all of the ingredients for the Beef Stew with Assorted Vegetable recipe for July 13, he can purchase the correct quantity of product. Based on the price paid for each ingredient, Sammy can determine a recipe cost for the 17 portions and a cost per portion. The current prices for the ingredients are listed below, along with their quantities.

| *Ingredient* | *Current Price* | *Quantity in Recipe for 17* | *Item Cost* |
|---|---|---|---|
| Beef chuck, cubed | $1.25 per pound | 8.5 lbs. × $1.25 = | $10.625 |
| Onions | $0.39 per pound | 2.125 lbs. × $0.39 = | $ 0.829 |
| Baby carrots | $0.79 per pound | 4.25 lbs. × $0.79 = | $ 3.358 |
| Celery | $0.69 per pound | 2.125 lbs. × $0.69 = | $ 1.466 |
| Green peas | $0.99 per pound | 2.125 lbs. × $0.99 = | $ 2.104 |
| Beef stock | $0.65 per quart | 4.25 qts. × $0.65 = | $ 2.763 |
| | | Total Cost for 17 portions | $21.145 |

Cost per portion:
$21.15 (rounded recipe cost) / 17 (portions) = $1.24

It costs Sammy $1.24 for every portion of Beef Stew with Assorted Vegetables served in his restaurant.

The actual costing of a "real" recipe is a little more complicated because there are some ingredients that are used in such a small quantity that it becomes very cumbersome to figure out an exact product cost. Examples of ingredients used in small quantities are herbs, spices, and perhaps oil in the deep-fat fryer. Herbs can be purchased fresh by the bunch or dried by the ounce or pound. Spices are purchased by the ounce or pound. Generally, a very small quantity of the bunch, ounce, or pound is used per recipe, so how cost effective is it to spend a great deal of time to arrive at a product cost? How much is one bay leaf or six peppercorns?

There are two methods used to account for miscellaneous ingredients in food service. One method is to figure out an annual cost for herbs, spices, and oil for the deep-fat fryers. The annual total is then divided by 12, and 1/12 of the annual cost is added to each month's total food cost. If Sammy's by the Seaside is using this method, Sammy would figure out how much was spent over a 12-month period for herbs, spices, and oil for the deep-fat fryers. Let's say Sammy spent $1,200.00 last year on these products. Sammy would divide the total by 12 (there are 12 months in one year), and get a cost per month for herbs, spices, and oil for the deep-fat fryers.

$1,200.00 (total cost for the year) / 12 (months)
= $100.00 per month

The $100.00 per month is added to the monthly food cost as the month-end financial statements are being prepared.

The second method for allocating the cost for herbs, spices, and oil for the deep-fat fryers is to add a certain percentage to the cost of each recipe. Let's say Sammy has decided to change the way he figures out the cost for herbs, spices, and oil for the deep-fat fryers. Sammy has decided to add a certain percentage to each recipe's cost to cover the cost of miscellaneous ingredients. Sammy decided that an additional 2 percent added to each recipe is a valid percentage. Sammy is going to begin with the recipe for Beef Stew with Assorted Vegetables.

The recipe Sammy costed out earlier was without seasonings, but the actual recipe uses salt, pepper, bay leaves, and thyme. The recipe cost for the 17 portions is $21.15. Sammy can add the additional 2 percent in one of two ways. He can multiply the recipe cost by 2 percent (.02) and then add the 2 percent to the total cost:

$21.15 (recipe cost) × .02 (2%) = $0.42

Then:

$21.15 (recipe cost) + $0.42
(the 2% for miscellaneous ingredients) = $21.57 new recipe cost

Or, Sammy can multiply the original recipe cost by 102 percent:

$21.15 (recipe cost) × 1.02 (102%) = $21.57 new recipe cost

The slight increase in the recipe cost creates a slight increase in the portion cost, too.

$21.57 (new recipe cost) / 17 (portions) = $1.27 new portion cost

The revised portion cost is $1.27.

Another issue that Sammy (and you) need to be aware of when costing a recipe is the unit of measure. If you review the beef stew recipe, every ingredient was purchased and used in the same unit of measure. This will not always be the case. Ingredients will always be purchased in a specific unit of measure, such as pound, gallon, liter, count per pound, or count per case. Some recipes' quantities will be listed in the purchasing unit of measure and some will not.

It is possible that an item purchased by the pound is used in a recipe measured in a fluid-ounce container—for example, 1 cup of flour or sugar. It is also possible that an item purchased by the liter is used by the cup in a recipe. In these instances, the conversion of the different purchasing to recipe units needs to be addressed before the recipe can be accurately costed out. There are conversion charts available that compare the differing units and assist us with the costing of a recipe. Most of the conversions are a close approximation of actual weight or volume, but they are close enough to arrive at an accurate recipe cost.

However, all of the time spent on recipe and portion costing is wasted if portion control is not used each time a guest is served.

## PORTIONS IN FOOD SERVICE

The size of the portion served to the guest varies based on a number of factors. The first factor is the meal period. Lunch portions are smaller than dinner portions. Some restaurants offer the same entrees for both lunch and dinner. The dinner portions are larger than the same item at lunch and might come with a choice of soup or salad. If this is the case, the menu price for the dinner entree is higher than the comparable entree served for lunch.

In a restaurant where the norm for dinner is a five-course meal, the size of the entree is probably smaller than the one in the above example. In this dining situation, the guest is served an appetizer, a soup, an intermezzo, the entree, and then a salad. If the size of the entree is too large, it has the chance of ending up in a "doggie bag" or worse (the garbage can).

Some food service operators check the garbage can during service. The can tells you what the customers did not like or could not finish. If there are certain entrees that always end up in the can, perhaps the portion size is too large.

The size of the portion varies by the market or the clientele the operation is trying to attract. Recent news stories focus on the "super-sized" meals offered at every fast-food outlet. Many fast-food customers opt for these super-sized meals. A casino hotel company in Las Vegas used to offer its buffet customers the "Plate of Plenty." The plastic plate had three sections and was 16 inches in diameter. Some customers are looking for quantity, while others are looking for quality.

What is the "average" portion size? The average portion size is what your restaurant develops its recipes to serve. The portion size for a protein item—for example, ahi tuna—could be 4 ounces, for a rib eye steak, it might be 8 ounces. The portion size will vary; the cost per portion is what matters. It must be determined based on the cost to prepare and serve that particular portion size. Once the recipes are developed and a portion cost is determined, we must ensure that the correct portion size is served to the guest.

There are many ways to control portion size. The easiest way is by the size of the service ware. Soup has to be served in a soup cup or bowl. A soup cup holds 4 fluid ounces and a bowl holds 8 fluid ounces. There is not any possible way to overportion soup. Glasses, paper cups, and coffee cups are similar to soup cups and bowls with regard to portioning. You cannot serve a portion larger than the container size.

Plates can be purchased in many different sizes. A dinner plate has a diameter of 10 inches with a decorative lip around the edge. The actual "plating" area is only 8 inches. A luncheon plate has a diameter that is 8 or 9 inches. The decorative lip leaves an actual "plating" area at 6 to 7 inches. Smaller-size plates are available for salads and desserts.

The back of the house can control portion size by using ladles, scoops, and scales. Once a portion size has been determined, the proper size ladle or scoop can be used to correctly portion the food items served to guests. If sliced meats are serviced, a portion-control scale can be used. All of these techniques ensure the amount of food we serve to the guest has the correct menu price to cover the cost of the food, other operating expenses, and our profit.

The production forecast estimates the number of covers of each menu item that our customers will order per meal period, per day. The standardized recipe produces a standard yield. Many food service operators with a static menu and a fairly consistent customer count think the development of a production forecast is a waste of time. However, time spent reviewing the sales history from last year and the recent past is time well spent prior to purchasing products and scheduling employees. This way there are no unexpected surprises because of a craft fair or a three-day weekend. The wise and successful operators review their forecasts and compare it to their product usage and labor cost.

## PRODUCTION PLANNING AND CONTROL REVIEW PROBLEMS

1. Why is production forecasting so important to a food service operation?

2. Why should the prior year and the past five weeks' sales history be considered in preparing a production forecast?

3. What is a standardized recipe?

4. What is a recipe yield?

5. How can a recipe yield be changed?

6. What is the procedure for developing a recipe cost?

7. What is the procedure for determining a portion cost?

8. Why is portion control so important to a food service operation?

9. Sales History: The following are the customer counts for lunch for the past five Thursdays.

| *Week* | *Customer Count* |
|---|---|
| 5 | 72 |
| 4 | 68 |
| 3 | 96 |
| 2 | 102 |
| 1 | 85 |

Last year on this date, the customer count for lunch was 57.

a. What general information can be developed from this sales history?

b. Is the sales history from last year useful in this case?

c. Using the last five weeks' customer counts, what is the forecast for customers for next Thursday?

**10.** Forecasted sales: Use the forecasted customer count from problem 9c and the following sales percentages:

| *Lunch Menu* | *Sales Percentage* |
|---|---|
| Item 1 | 18% |
| Item 2 | 29% |
| Item 3 | 37% |
| Item 4 | 16% |

a. What is the sales forecast for each of these menu items?

b. Based on the forecasted menu item sales, and an original recipe yield for each item of 8, what is the multiplier/conversion factor for each menu item recipe?

**11.** Recipe cost: Using the following recipe quantities and product cost:

Example Recipe Yield: 20 portions

| *Quantity* | *Product* | *Item Cost* |
|---|---|---|
| 2 lbs. | Ground beef | $ 1.59 per pound |
| 3 lbs. | Dry kidney beans | $ 0.69 per pound |
| 1 lb. | Onions | $ 0.59 per pound |
| .5 lb. | Green chili peppers | $ 0.89 per pound |

a. What is the cost for this recipe?

b. What is the cost per portion?

c. What is the recipe cost if we add 2 percent for seasonings?

d. What is the new portion cost?

## Production Planning and Control Review Answers

1. Production forecasting increases the operations planning and control. It creates a smarter purchasing and scheduling routine.
2. Past sales history contains valuable information about customer count and menu item selection.
3. A standardized recipe is a list of quantities, ingredients, and preparation methods that, if followed, produce a consistent product with a consistent yield and a consistent cost.
4. A recipe yield is the quantity of product that a recipe produces. The yield can be a certain quantity, like 2 gallons, or a number of portions.
5. A recipe yield can be changed by adjusting all of the ingredients by an equal amount. The adjustment amount is determined by the following formula:

$$\frac{\text{New yield}}{\text{Old yield}} = \text{Multiplier or conversion factor}$$

6. A recipe cost is determined by multiplying each ingredient by its AP price per unit.
7. A portion cost is determined by dividing a recipe cost by its yield in portions.
8. Portion control is important in food service because our forecast, purchasing, recipe cost, portion cost, and menu price are based on the portion sizes developed.
9. Sales history
   a. Business has picked up over the last three Thursdays.
   b. No, because the customer count is lower than the past five Thursdays.
   c. Develop an average for the last five weeks:

$72 + 68 + 96 + 102 + 85 = 423 \quad 423 / 5 = 84.6$ rounded to 85

10. Forecasted sales:
    a. Item 1: 85 (customer count) × .18 (18%) = 15.3 rounded to 16
    Item 2: 85 (customer count) × .29 (29%) = 24.7 rounded to 25
    Item 3: 85 (customer count) × .37 (37%) = 31.5 rounded to 32
    Item 4: 85 (customer count) × .16 (16%) = 13.6 rounded to 14
    Total: 87 due to rounding

b. Recipe yield multiplier/conversion factor
Item 1: 16 / 8 = 2
Item 2: 25 / 8 = 3.125
Item 3: 32 / 8 = 4
Item 4: 14 / 8 = 1.75

**11.** Recipe cost:

a.

| | | |
|---|---|---|
| Ground beef | 2 lbs. × $1.59 per pound | = $3.18 |
| Kidney beans | 3 lbs. × $0.69 per pound | = $2.07 |
| Onions | 1 lb. × $0.59 per pound | = $0.59 |
| Chili peppers | .5 lb. × $0.89 per pound | = $0.445 |
| | Total Recipe Cost: | $6.285 |

b. $6.285 (recipe cost) / 20 (portions) = $0.314 cost per portion

c. $6.285 × 1.02 (102%) = $6.41 Recipe cost with seasonings added as 2% of total

d. $6.41 (new recipe cost) / 20 (portions) = $0.32 cost per portion

# Chapter 7
# MENU PRICING

The pricing of the menu is perhaps one of the most important mathematical functions we perform in a food service operation, although menu pricing is not based on true mathematics. There are many factors that extend menu pricing beyond the simple answer to an equation. These factors include the need to make a profit, the customers' perception of value for the price, the location of the operation, the quality of the food, and the expertise of the staff.

The menu price for each item should consider the variety of costs/expenses that a food service operation has, as well as the need to earn a "fair" profit. The categories of operating and capital expenses in a food service operation can be seen in this profit and loss statement (P&L), commonly known as an income statement. This P&L/income statement is for Thomas Morgan's Great Steaks and is for the month of June 20XX.

As you can see from the P&L, the sales revenue collected from selling our menu items goes to pay many operating and capital expenses before we can see how much profit has been earned. All of these expenses are a necessary cost of doing business for a food service operation and need to be paid. So how do we price our menu so that there is enough revenue to cover all of these costs and still make a profit? There are many answers to that question. First, however, let's review the terminology used in menu pricing.

**Thomas Morgan's Great Steaks**
**Profit and Loss Statement**
**(Income Statement)**
**June 20XX**

| | *Dollars* | *Percentage* |
|---|---|---|
| Sales Revenue | | |
| Food | $40,000.00 | 80% |
| Beverage | $10,000.00 | 20% |
| Total Revenue | $50,000.00 | 100% |
| | | |
| Cost of Sales | | |
| Cost of Food | $14,000.00 | 35% of $40,000 (food cost) |
| Cost of Beverage | $2,000.00 | 20% of $10,000 (beverage cost |
| Total Cost of Sales | $16,000.00 | |
| [$50,000.00 (total revenue) − $16,000.00 (total sales) = $34,000.00] | | |
| Gross Profit | $34,000.00 | |
| | | |
| Operating Expenses | | |
| Salaries and Wages | $12,000.00 | 24% of $50,000 (direct labor cost) |
| Employee Benefits | $3,000.00 | 6% of $50,000 (benefit cost) |
| China, Glassware, Flatware, Linens | $50.00 | |
| Cleaning Supplies | $295.00 | |
| Uniforms | $525.00 | |
| Menus | $0.00 | |
| Paper Products | $400.00 | |
| Administrative and General | $255.00 | |
| Marketing and Advertising | $50.00 | |
| Operations and Maintenance | $325.00 | |
| Utilities | $1,200.00 | |
| Total Operating Expenses | $18,100.00 | |
| [$34,000.00 (gross profit) − $18,100.00 (total operating expenses) = $15,900.00] | | |
| Income Before Capital Expenses | $15,900.00 | |
| | | |
| Capital Expenses | | |
| Insurance | $750.00 | |
| Rent | $4,000.00 | |
| Real Estate Taxes | $800.00 | |
| Interest Expense | $1,450.00 | |
| Depreciation | $2,900.00 | |
| | | |
| Total Capital Expenses | $9,900.00 | |
| [$15,900.00 (income before capital expenses) − $9,900.00 (capital expenses) = $6,000.00] | | |
| Profit Before Income Taxes | $6,000.00 | |

## PRICING TERMINOLOGY

Classical culinary techniques are deeply rooted in France, and so are the terms used to describe exactly what the customer receives for the price stated on the menu. French terminology used in menu pricing is a la carte, table d'hote, or prix fixe. A la carte means each item listed on the menu is priced individually. Table d'hote and/or prix fixe means that the entire meal is included in the price. Let's look at the two menus below to see the difference between a true a la carte menu and a true table d'hote or prix fixe menu.

**Thomas Morgan's Great Steaks**

| A La Carte Menu | Table d'Hote or Prix Fixe Menu |
|---|---|
| 12 oz. Prime Rib Eye Steak<br>$29.95 | All dinners include<br>salad, baked potato,<br>and vegetable du jour |
| Russet Baked Potato served with<br>your choice of toppings<br>$6.95 | 12 oz Choice Rib Eye<br>$18.95 |
| Fresh Vegetable du Jour<br>$8.95 | |
| Seasonal Garden Salad<br>$8.95 | |
| Total cost for dinner: $54.80 | $18.95 |

$54.80 (a la carte menu price)
− $18.95 (table d'hote menu price) = $35.85

The difference in the price for a meal at the restaurant that prices the menu using a la carte pricing versus the restaurant that uses table d'hote/prix fixe pricing is $35.85. The meal on the a la carte menu is almost three times the price of the meal on the table d'hote menu. What is the difference in these two menus?

The most obvious difference is in the quality of the steak. The steak that is priced a la carte is a USDA prime cut of beef, whereas the steak that is priced table d'hote is a USDA choice cut of beef. The potato on the a la carte menu is a russet, whereas there is no description on the table d'hote menu. Besides these two differences, what else would justify the huge difference in the price of these two steak dinners?

The difference would be in the location of the restaurant, the ambiance of the dining room, the quality of the service, and the market or type of customer the restaurant can attract. Businesspeople who are entertaining a client will pay a la carte prices. People celebrating a special occasion will pay a la carte prices. People who want to experience the "best" will pay a la carte prices.

Many customers would be very satisfied to eat the steak dinner at the table d'hote restaurant. This restaurant might be located in the neighborhood close to where customers live. They can be regular customers who visit often because the price is more affordable. Menu pricing must take into consideration many factors beyond the cost of the food. Although the cost of the food is a critical piece of information, that must be known before the menu price is determined.

## PORTION COST AND PLATE COST

The cost to serve the guest a portion or plate is still a basic "ingredient" in the search to properly price the menu. Portion costs and plate costs come from the price we pay for our products, the yield on the product, the recipe cost, and the portion size and cost. In addition, when we actually "plate" the food, any garnish or decorating of the plate that we use is an additional cost that somehow needs to be factored into the menu price. If the garnish is a piece of parsley, then the cost is insignificant, but if the garnish is a sauce, such as a coulis, that is skillfully used to decorate the plate, then the cost of food and labor must be considered.

## FOOD-COST PERCENTAGE

The food-cost percentage is a mathematical comparison of the cost of the food compared to its selling price. A food-cost percentage can be determined for each item on the menu, or an aggregate food-cost percentage can be determined for total food cost and total food sales by day, week, month, or year:

$$\frac{\text{Cost of food}}{\text{Menu price (for each item on the menu)}} = \text{Food-cost percentage}$$

*or*

$$\frac{\text{Cost of food}}{\text{Sales revenue (for the day, week, month, or year)}} = \text{Food-cost percentage}$$

Using the steak menus from Thomas Morgan's Great Steaks and the price list and portion size below, let's see how a food-cost percentage is determined.

| *Rib Eye* | *AP Price* | *Yield %* | *Portion Size* |
|---|---|---|---|
| Prime Rib Eye | $5.95 a pound | Portion control | 12 oz. |
| Choice Rib Eye | $3.95 a pound | Portion control | 12 oz. |
| *Potatoes* | | | |
| Russet, 35 count | $35.00 case | Portion control | 1 each |
| Russet, 80 count | $20.00 case | Portion control | 1 each |
| *Vegetable du Jour* | | | |
| Asparagus, small | $ 1.99 pound (15 spears) | Portion control | 5 spears |
| Broccoli | $ 0.99 pound | 62.8% | 4 oz. |
| *Salad* | | | |
| Iceberg lettuce | $25.00 cs (24 heads) | 280 portions/cs | 2 oz |
| Assorted lettuce mix | $20.00 cs (4/2.5# bags) | 100% | 8 oz. |

First we need to determine the plate cost for each of our menu items. Beginning with the a la carte menu:

The prime rib eye steak is purchased by the pound, and the portion size is 12 ounces.

$5.95 (cost per pound) / 16 (ounces per pound) = $0.372 per ounce

$0.372 (cost per pound) × 12 (ounces per serving) = $4.46 portion cost

*or*

12 oz. (portion size) / 16 oz. (purchase unit) = ¾, .75, or 75%

Therefore, the portion cost is ¾, .75, or 75 percent of the per-pound cost.

$5.95 (price per pound) × .75 (portion percentage of a pound) = $4.46 portion cost

The 12 ounce prime rib eye steak costs $4.46. The menu price is $29.95. The food-cost percentage for this item is:

$4.46 / $29.95 = .149, or 14.9%, rounded to 15%

What does a food-cost percentage tell us? It tells us that for every dollar we collect selling a 12-ounce prime rib eye steak for $29.95,

15 cents (.15 or 15%) covers the cost of the steak. If 15 cents covers the cost of the steak, then 85 cents (.85 or 85%) is left from each sales dollar to cover the operating and capital expenses and the profit.

The next menu item from the a la carte menu is the russet potato. The russets are packed 35 potatoes to a case, and the case price is $35.00. Each potato costs:

$35.00 (case price) / 35 (potatoes) = $1.00 per potato

The menu price for the russet potato is $6.95. The food-cost percentage for this item is:

$1.00 (cost per potato) / $6.95 (menu price) = .1439, or 14.39%

The food-cost percentage can be rounded to 14%. This means that 14 cents (.14 or 14%) of every dollar collected from selling the russet potato covers the cost of the potato. The remaining 86 cents (.86 or 86%) from every dollar collected covers the operating and capital costs and the profit.

When a guest orders a baked potato, it is common for butter, sour cream, chives, bacon bits, and/or other items to be used as a topping. The cost of these toppings must be factored into the plate cost and the food-cost percentage. These costs have not been considered in this example.

The next menu item from the a la carte menu is the fresh vegetable du jour. Asparagus is the vegetable du jour. It is purchased by the pound, and one pound is 15 spears. One portion is 5 spears. The portion cost is:

$1.99 (price per pound) / 15 (spears per pound)
= $0.133 per spear

$0.133 (price per spear) × 5 (spears per portion)
= $0.665 per portion

*or*

5 (spears per portion) / 15 (spears per pound) = ⅓, .333, or 33%

$1.99 (price per pound) × .333 (portion percentage of a pound) = $0.663 cost per portion (rounding is responsible for the difference in totals)

The menu price for the vegetable du jour is $8.95. The food cost percentage is

$0.663 (cost per portion) / $8.95 (menu price) = .0741, or 7.41%

The food-cost percentage can be rounded to 7 percent. This means that 7 cents (.07 or 7%) of every dollar collected from selling the vegetable du jour covers the cost of the vegetable. The remaining 93 cents (.93 or 93%) covers the operating and capital expenses and the profit.

The last item on the a la carte menu is the seasonal garden salad. The salad is made with the assorted lettuce mix. The assorted lettuce mix is packed 4/2.5 pound bags per case. The case price is $20.00. The portion size is 8 ounces.

One case contains four bags of assorted mix lettuce. Each bag weighs 2.5 pounds. Therefore, one case contains

4 (bags) × 2.5 (pounds per bag)
= 10 pounds of assorted lettuce mix per case

One case costs $20.00. What is the cost per pound of assorted lettuce mix?

$20.00 (cost per case) / 10 (pounds per case)
= $2.00 per pound of assorted lettuce mix

The portion size is 8 ounces. The portion cost is figured this way:

$2.00 (cost per pound) / 16 (ounces per pound) = $0.125 per ounce

$0.125 (cost per ounce) × 8 (portion size) = $1.00 per portion

*or*

8 (ounces) / 16 (ounces) = 1/2, .50, or 50%

Therefore, the portion cost is 1/2, .50, or 50 percent of the per pound price.

$ 2.00 (cost per pound) × .50 = $1.00 cost per portion

The menu price for the seasonal garden salad is $8.95. The food-cost percentage is:

$1.00 (portion cost) / $8.95 (menu price) = .1117, or 11.17%

The food-cost percentage can be rounded to 11%. This means that 11 cents (.11 or 11%) of every dollar collected selling the seasonal garden salad covers the cost of the assorted lettuce mix. The remaining 89 cents (.89 or 89%) covers the operating and capital costs and the profit.

The overall food-cost percentage for an entire steak dinner from the a la carte menu looks like this:

| *Menu Item* | *Portion Cost* | *Menu Price* | *Formula* | *Food-Cost Percentage* |
|---|---|---|---|---|
| Prime Rib Eye | \$4.46 | \$29.95 | (4.46 / 29.95) × 100 | 14.90% |
| Russet Potato | \$1.00 | \$ 6.95 | (1.00 / 6.96) × 100 | 14.39% |
| Vegetable du Jour | \$0.66 | \$ 8.95 | (.66 / 8.95) × 100 | 7.41% |
| Seasonal Garden Salad | \$1.00 | \$ 8.95 | (1.00 / 8.95) × 100 | 11.71% |
| Total | \$7.12 | \$54.80 | | |

\$7.12 (total food cost) / \$54.80 (total menu price)
= .1299 or 12.99, rounded to 13%

The overall food-cost percentage of 13 percent means that for every customer who orders a complete dinner, 13 cents (.13 or 13%) of every sales dollar covers the cost of the food, and 87 cents (.87 or 87%) of every sales dollar covers the operating and capital expenses and the profit.

.13 (food cost percentage) × \$54.80 (total menu price)
= \$7.12 total food-cost

*and*

.87 (gross profit per dollar) × \$54.80 (total menu price)
= \$47.68 total gross profit

The a la carte menu used in this example yields a low overall food-cost percentage of 13 percent and a high overall gross profit margin of 87 percent. This is because the menu prices are high, compared to the cost of the food.

Let's compare this a la carte menu to the table d'hote (prix fixe) menu. The table d'hote (prix fixe) menu prices the entire meal at one price. Therefore, there is only one food-cost percentage. It is for the entire meal.

The choice rib eye steak is purchased by the pound, and the portion size is 12 ounces.

\$3.95 (cost per pound) / 16 (ounces per pound) = \$0.247 per ounce

\$0.247 (cost per ounce) × 12 (ounces per portion)
= \$2.96 per serving

*or*

12 (ounces per portion) / 16 (ounces per pound)
= ¾, .75, or 75%

Therefore, the portion cost is ¾, .75, or 75 percent of the cost per pound.

\$3.95 (cost per pound) × .75 (portion percentage of a pound)
= \$2.96 per serving

The next menu item is the potato. These russet potatoes are packed 80 to a case. A case costs \$20.00. What is the cost per potato?

\$20.00 (cost per case) / 80 (potatoes per case) = \$0.25 per potato

This potato would also be served with toppings such as butter, sour cream, chives, bacon bits, and/or with other toppings. The cost of the toppings needs to be factored into the cost of serving the baked potato.

The next menu item is the vegetable du jour. On this menu, the vegetable du jour is broccoli. Broccoli is purchased by the pound and has a 62.8-percent yield. The portion size is 4 ounces.

\$0.99 (cost per AP pound) / .628 (yield percentage)
= \$1.576 per EP pound

\$1.576 (cost per EP pound) / 16 (ounces per pound)
= \$0.0985 per ounce

\$0.0985 (cost per ounce) × 4 (ounces per portion)
= \$0.394 per portion

*or*

4 (ounces per portion) / 16 (ounces per pound) = ¼, .25, or 25%

Therefore, the portion cost is ¼, .25, or 25 percent of the EP cost per pound.

\$1.576 (EP cost per pound) × .25 (portion percentage of a pound)
= \$0.39 per portion

The last item on the table d'hote (prix fixe) menu is the salad. The salad is an iceberg lettuce salad. Iceberg lettuce is purchased by the case, and a case yields 280 2-ounce salads.

\$25.00 (cost per case) / 280 (portions per case)
= \$0.089, or \$0.09 per salad

The overall food-cost percentage for the table d'hote (prix fixe) menu is:

| *Menu Item* | *Portion Cost* | *Menu Price* | *Formula* | *Food-Cost Percentage* |
|---|---|---|---|---|
| Choice Rib Eye | \$2.96 | | | |
| Russet Potato | \$0.25 | | | |
| Vegetable du Jour | \$0.39 | | | |
| Salad | \$0.09 | | | |
| Total | \$3.69 | \$18.95 | (3.69 / 18.95) × 100 | 19.5% |

\$3.69 (total food cost) / \$18.95 (menu price) = .195 or 19.5%

The food-cost percentage of 19.5 percent means that for every customer that purchases the choice rib eye dinner, 19.5 cents (.195 or 19.5%) of every sales dollar goes to cover the cost of the food and 80.5 cents (.805 or 80.5%) of every sales dollar goes to cover the operating and capital costs and to the profit.

.195 (food-cost percentage) × \$18.95 (menu price)
= \$3.70 total food cost

*and*

.805 (gross profit per dollar) × \$18.95 (menu price)
= \$15.25 total gross profit

The table d'hote (prix fixe) menu yields a food-cost percentage of 19.5 percent and a gross-profit percentage of 80.5 percent. The 19.5 percent food-cost percentage is higher than the 13 percent for the a la carte menu but is still a respectable percentage by industry standards.

The most notable difference between these two menus is the amount of money left over after the cost of the food is covered. On the a la carte menu, \$47.68 is available to cover other expenses, whereas on the table d'hote (prix fixe) menu, \$15.25 is available to cover the other expenses. The question is, can these restaurants make a profit based on their food-cost percentages, gross-profit percentages, and their customer base?

## AVERAGE GUEST CHECK

The *average guest check* is a term used to describe how much money the average customer spends in our restaurant. In this example, we have two different steak houses. One is an upscale steak house with an average guest check of $54.80 and the other is a casual steak house with an average guest check of $18.95. In this example we have identical profit and loss statements for our two restaurants. I realize this is a statistically impossible, but please follow along with me.

The sales revenue for our two steak houses is $40,000.00. If the average guest check for our upscale steak house is $54.80, how many customers did we serve?

$40,000.00 (total food sales) / $54.80 (average guest check)
= 729.927, rounded to 730

We served 730 customers in the month of June 20XX at our upscale steak house.

If the average guest check at our casual steak house is $18.95, how many customers did we serve?

$40,000.00 (total food sales) / $18.95 (average guest check)
= 2,110.8, rounded to 2,111

We served 2,111 customers in the month of June 20XX at our casual steak house.

Would you rather have an upscale steak house with very low volume and a high gross profit, or a casual steak house with a slightly lower gross profit but much higher volume? The higher the menu prices are, the smaller the number of customers that will regularly come to visit your restaurant, generally speaking.

## HOW TO PRICE A MENU

When you begin to price a menu, all of the factors mentioned previously must be taken into account: the need to make a profit, the customers' perception of value for the price, the location of the operation, the quality of the food, and the expertise of the staff. Then we turn to the mathematics. Exactly how much money is needed monthly to pay for all of the operating and capital expenses and the profit?

After we have our monthly expenses, we can make an educated estimate of the number of customers that will dine with us on a monthly basis. We need to make this estimation for each meal period we serve. Then we can determine what dollar value we need for our average guest check. From there, we determine our menu price.

Warren decides to open a restaurant. He works with a professional real-estate person and finds a location that costs $30,000.00 a year for rent, real-estate taxes, insurance, and utilities. Warren knows that the cost per month is

$30,000.00 (cost per year) / 12 (months per year)
= $2,500.00 a month

In addition to those expenses, Warren determines his salaries, benefits, and all other operating expenses will be an additional $5,000.00 a month. Now Warren has operating and capital expenses of $7,500.00. Warren would like to earn $5,000.00 a month. Now he needs to generate $12,500.00 in sales just to cover the operating and capital costs and his profit.

Warren determines that he would like to have an average guest check of $15.00. He plans on running a 30-percent food cost. A 30-percent food cost means that the average cost of food is .30 of every dollar of the menu price. It also means that Warren will run a 70-percent gross profit margin.

If 70 percent of Warren's revenue have to equal $12,500.00 monthly, then how much money does he have to generate to run a 30-percent food-cost percentage?

$12,500.00 (monthly operating, capital and profit)
/ .70 (gross profit %) = $17,857.14 in sales

If he plans on having a $15.00 average guest check, how many customers does he need to serve monthly?

$17,857.14 (monthly sales) / $15.00 (average guest check)
= 1,190 customers monthly

If Warren can indeed have about 1,200 customers walk in his restaurant and spend, on average, $15.00, then he can begin to price his menu. Warren would determine the cost to serve a guest an item based on purchase cost, product yield, recipe cost, and portion size. Then Warren would determine the menu price based on a 30-percent food-cost percentage (the food service industry average for food-cost percentage is 30%):

$$\frac{\text{Cost of food}}{\text{Food cost percentage}} = \text{Menu price}$$

Warren has six menu items:

| *Item* | *Food Cost* | *Food-Cost Percentage* | *Formula* | *Menu Price* |
|---|---|---|---|---|
| A | $4.29 | 30% (.30) | (4.29/.30) | $14.30 |
| B | $5.50 | 30% (.30) | (5.50/.30) | $18.33 |

| *Item* | *Food Cost* | *Food-Cost Percentage* | *Formula* | *Menu Price* |
|---|---|---|---|---|
| C | $3.72 | 30% (.30) | (3.72/.30) | $12.40 |
| D | $6.46 | 30% (.30) | (6.46/.30) | $21.53 |
| E | $2.50 | 30% (.30) | (2.50/.30) | $ 8.33 |
| F | $3.99 | 30% (.30) | (3.99/.30) | $13.30 |

Now that Warren has "priced" his menu based on a 30-percent food cost and a 70-percent gross profit margin, let's look at the prices to see if they need to be adjusted.

First, let us average the six prices to see how close they come to Warren's target of a $15.00 average guest check.

$$\$14.30 + \$18.33 + \$12.40 + \$21.53 + \$8.33 + \$13.30 = \$88.19$$

$$\$88.19 / 6 = \$14.698$$

Warren is very close to his target guest check, but as he adjusts his prices, he might choose to round up to raise his average from $14.698 to $15.00.

The first thing Warren needs to look at is the spread between the highest- and lowest-priced items. The difference between $21.53 and $8.33 is

$$\$21.53 - \$8.33 = \$13.20$$

That is too great of a price spread, because it might "suggest" to some customers that the $21.00 item is too expensive. So Warren will adjust the $21.53 item to $19.95 and the $8.33 item to $11.95. Then the spread is reduced and the customers will tend to order based on choice, not price.

The other prices need to be adjusted as well. Generally, menu items end in the digit 5. This is based on consumer pricing psychology.

Warren might adjust his prices like this:

| *Item* | *Food-Cost Percentage Price* | *Adjusted Price* |
|---|---|---|
| A | $14.30 | $15.95 |
| B | $18.33 | $17.95 |
| C | $12.40 | $12.95 |
| D | $21.53 | $19.95 |
| E | $ 8.33 | $11.95 |
| F | $13.30 | $14.95 |

When Warren averages his adjusted menu prices, his new average is

$$\$15.95 + \$17.95 + \$12.95 + \$19.95 + \$11.95 + \$14.95 = \$93.70$$

$$\$93.70 / 6 = \$15.62$$

Warren has adjusted his menu prices after he used a 30-percent food-cost percentage to determine approximately what they should be. By adjusting the prices, he has raised his mathematical average and he has eliminated price shopping by his customers. *That* is how to price a menu.

## MENU PRICING: REVIEW PROBLEMS

1. Why is menu pricing so important to a food service operation?

2. What factors affect menu prices?

3. What is a profit and loss statement/income statement?

4. What kind of information is contained in a P&L/income statement?

5. Why is this information useful in menu pricing?

6. What does *a la carte* mean?

7. What does *table d'hote/prix fixe* mean?

8. What is the formula for an individual menu item's food-cost percentage?

9. What is the formula for an aggregate (daily, weekly, monthly, or annual) food-cost percentage?

10. What formula would you use to price a menu at a predetermined food-cost percentage?

11. What is an average guest check?

12. Use the following P&L/income statement:

**Skinny Minnie's Low-Fat Delights**
**Profit and Loss Statement**
**October 20XX**

| | |
|---|---|
| Sales Revenue | |
| Food | $57,250.00 |
| Beverage | 12,800.00 |
| Total | $70,050.00 |

| | |
|---|---|
| Cost of Sale | |
| Food | $16,320.00 |
| Beverage | 2,899.00 |
| Total | $19,219.00 |

a. What is the aggregate food-cost percentage?

b. What is the aggregate beverage-cost percentage?

c. If we served 3,545 customers at Skinny Minnie's in October, what is the average guest check for food sales?

d. What is the average guest check for beverage sales?

**13.** Food-Cost Percentage: Use the following information:

| *Item* | *AP Cost* | *Portion Size* |
|---|---|---|
| I | $ 2.99 per pound | 6 ounces |
| II | $ 3.49 per pound | 10 ounces |
| III | $ 5.99 per pound | 4 ounces |

a. What is the cost per portion?

b. If the menu price for Items I, II, and III is $9.95, what is the respective food-cost percentage?

c. If the desired food-cost percentage for Items I, II, and III is 25 percent, what is the new menu price?

**14.** Menu price adjustment: A new menu is being planned. The menu prices for the items at the predetermined food-cost percentage are as follows:

| | |
|---|---|
| Entree S | $13.42 |
| Entree P | $15.67 |
| Entree R | $ 8.90 |
| Entree I | $17.14 |
| Entree N | $22.43 |
| Entree G | $11.11 |

a. What is the spread between the highest and lowest price?

b. Is the spread too large? Why or why not?

c. How could these prices be adjusted?

## Menu Pricing: Review Question Answers

1. Menu pricing determines the revenue stream (cash flow), the customer base, the quality of the food served, and the expertise of the employees.
2. The factors that affect menu prices are product cost, operating expenses, capital costs, customer base, and local competition.
3. A profit and loss statement/income statement is a list of all revenue collected and all expenses incurred by a business.
4. The kind of information contained in a P&L is food and beverage sales, food and beverage cost, payroll expense, utilities, advertising, uniforms, china, glass, rent, insurance, and so on, and hopefully, a profit and not a loss.
5. The information contained in the P&L provides us with our costs of doing business. Menu prices and customer counts must be able to pay for all of these costs.
6. A la carte means each item on the menu is sold separately, has its own price.
7. Table d'hote/prix fixe means that an entire meal is sold for one price.
8. The formula for an individual menu items food-cost percentage is:

$$\frac{\text{Cost of the menu item}}{\text{Menu price}} = \text{Food-cost percentage}$$

9. The formula for an aggregate (daily, weekly, monthly, or annual) food-cost percentage is:

$$\frac{\text{Aggregate food cost (for the day, week, month or year)}}{\text{Aggregate food sales (for the day, week, month or year)}} = \text{Overall food-cost percentage}$$

10. The formula to price an item at a predetermined food-cost percentage is:

$$\frac{\text{Food cost}}{\text{Predetermined food-cost percentage}} = \text{Menu price}$$

**11.** An average guest check is the amount of money an average customer spends in a restaurant.

**12.** Profit and Loss/income statement

a. Cost of food / Food sales $16,320 / $57,250 = 28.5%

b. Cost of beverage / Beverage sales
$ 2,899 / $12,800 = 22.65 rounded to 22.7%

c. Food sales / Customer count $57,259 / 3545 = $16.15

d. Beverage sales / Customer count
$12,800 / 3545 = $3.61

**13.** Food-Cost Percentage:

a. Item I $2.99 / 16 (ounces) = .1869 per ounce × 6 ounces = $1.12
Item II $3.49 / 16 (ounces) = .2181 per ounce × 10 ounces = $2.18
Item III $5.99 / 16 (ounces) = .3744 per ounce × 4 ounces = $1.50

b. Item I $1.12 (portion cost) / $9.95 (menu price) = .1126 or 11.3%
Item II $2.18 (portion cost) / $9.95 (menu price) = .2191 or 22%
Item III $1.50 (portion cost) / $9.95 (menu price) = .1508 or 15%

c. Item I $1.12 (portion cost) / .25 (predetermined food cost %) = $4.48
Item II $2.18 (portion cost) / .25 (predetermined food cost %) = $8.72
Item III $1.50 (portion cost) / .25 (predetermined food cost %) = $6.00

**14.** Menu Price Adjustment

a. Entree N is $22.43
Entree R is $ 8.90
The spread is the difference of $13.53.

b. The spread is large enough to "force" some customers to order based on price.

c. The adjustments should be in these ranges:
Entree S $12.95 to $14.95
Entree P $15.95
Entree R $9.95 to $12.95
Entree I $15.95 to $18.95
Entree N $19.95 to $21.95
Entree G $ 9.95 to $12.95

# Chapter 8

# LABOR COST AND CONTROL TECHNIQUES

The cost of labor is the highest operating expenses in a typical food service operation. Labor cost can average 30 to 35 percent of sales. In some operations, labor costs can be as high as 40 percent of sales. This means that for every dollar we collect in food sales, \$0.30 to \$0.35 or perhaps even \$0.40 is spent to cover the cost of labor.

$$\text{Labor-Cost Percentage} = \frac{\text{Total Labor Cost}}{\text{Total Sales Rev}}$$

The actual dollar amount paid to an employee is only the beginning of our labor costs. In many food service operations, employees are offered benefits. Benefits can include health, dental, and vision insurance; paid vacation; sick and bereavement leave; or even a retirement plan. The cost of these benefits is an additional expense to the employer. Then there are taxes.

The burden of tax collection and payment falls to the employer, the food service company. There is the cost associated with the mechanics of payroll and the disbursement of monies to the various governmental taxing agencies. The employer is liable for 50 percent of an employee's Social Security tax (FICA), and the entire federal (FUTA) and state (SUTA) tax for unemployment and injured worker's compensation. The employer is also liable to pay these taxes for monies earned as tips by food and beverage servers and bartenders.

The wise food service operator uses several techniques to ensure that the operation is properly staffed to meet the needs of the customers and payroll costs are kept at certain percentage of sales. The ability to control labor costs depends on many factors. The greatest influence on labor cost is organized labor. Organized labor means that the employees are represented by and are members of a union.

Culinary union membership is greatest in large metropolitan areas in the United States. Las Vegas, Miami, New York City, and San Francisco are examples of large metropolitan areas in the United States with large culinary union membership.

There are many advantages for members of a labor union. Generally speaking, union members earn a higher hourly wage and have a better benefit package than nonunion workers. Another advantage of union membership is an "almost" guarantee of a 40-hour work week.

Union membership increases the cost of labor for the food service operator. Union rules can makes it difficult or even impossible for a food service operator to practice some labor-control techniques. Therefore, it is crucial in a union "house" that we hire and schedule employees properly. Proper hiring and scheduling begins with a staffing guide.

## STAFFING GUIDE

A staffing guide is a chart or graph that indicates the number of employees needed based on the forecasted number of customers per hour. The chart or graph begins with zero customers and ends with the maximum number of customers that can be seated in the dining room at one time. The staffing guide balances zero customers with a "skeleton" staff that prepares the operation for the arrival of the customers and a "skeleton" staff that cleans the operation at the end of the day.

Employee scheduling is then based on the forecasted number of customers. There is a separate staffing guide for each job category. Job categories might include cashier, host/ess, food server, beverage server, bartender, sous chef, line cook, dishwasher, and so on.

At Anna's Annex, a dinner house, the dining room seats 200 guests. Anna's food servers can each serve up to 25 customers per hour. The maximum number of food servers that can work in the dining room is 8.

Below is the staffing guide for food servers for Anna's Annex. One food server comes in before the restaurant is open to prepare the service area. This server would ice the soft-drink machine; start the coffee; check the sugar, salt and peppers; and so on.

**Staffing Guide: Dining Room Servers**

| *Number of Customers* | *Number of Food Servers* |
|---|---|
| 0 | 1 |
| 1 to 25 | 1 |
| 26 to 50 | 2 |
| 51 to 75 | 3 |
| 76 to 100 | 4 |
| 101 to 125 | 5 |
| 126 to 150 | 6 |
| 151 to 175 | 7 |
| 176 to 200 | 8 |

At Anna's Annex, the line cooks can prepare food for up to 20 customers per hour. The maximum number of cooks that can work behind the line is five. Anna schedules two line cooks to come in before the restaurant opens in order to complete all of the necessary preparation.

**Staffing Guide: Line Cooks**

| *Number of Customers* | *Number of Line Cooks* |
|---|---|
| 0 | 2 |
| 1 to 40 | 2 |
| 41 to 60 | 3 |
| 61 to 80 | 4 |
| > than 81 | 5 |

The staffing guide assists with the scheduling of employees based on the needs of the customers. It assists with labor cost control because customer demand dictates employee schedules.

## EMPLOYEE SCHEDULES

The first step to employee scheduling is to forecast the number of customers that will visit the restaurant per meal period. Forecasting was explained in Chapter 6, "Production Planning and Control."

Here is the forecast for Anna's Annex for next week. Anna's Annex is a dinner house; therefore, Anna only staffs one meal period.

**Forecast of Customer Counts per Hour**

| | *Sunday* | *Monday* | *Tuesday* | *Wednesday* | *Thursday* | *Friday* | *Saturday* |
|---|---|---|---|---|---|---|---|
| 3 to 4 | 0 | 0 | 0 | 0 | 0 | 0 | 0 |
| 4 to 5 | 10 | 10 | 10 | 10 | 15 | 18 | 18 |
| 5 to 6 | 20 | 10 | 10 | 25 | 35 | 50 | 50 |
| 6 to 7 | 20 | 15 | 15 | 40 | 50 | 60 | 80 |
| 7 to 8 | 15 | 12 | 15 | 35 | 50 | 60 | 80 |
| 8 to 9 | 10 | 8 | 8 | 20 | 25 | 50 | 60 |
| 9 to 10 | 10 | 6 | 6 | 18 | 20 | 35 | 45 |
| 10 to 11 | 0 | 0 | 0 | 10 | 12 | 20 | 30 |

Utilizing the forecast and the staffing guide, Anna can plan a schedule for the food servers and line cooks. The number of employees needed to meet the customer demand is listed on this schedule.

**Schedule: Dining Room Servers**

| | *Sunday* | *Monday* | *Tuesday* | *Wednesday* | *Thursday* | *Friday* | *Saturday* |
|---|---|---|---|---|---|---|---|
| 3 to 4 | 1 | 1 | 1 | 1 | 1 | 1 | 1 |
| 4 to 5 | 1 | 1 | 1 | 1 | 1 | 1 | 1 |
| 5 to 6 | 1 | 1 | 1 | 1 | 2 | 2 | 2 |
| 6 to 7 | 1 | 1 | 1 | 2 | 2 | 3 | 4 |
| 7 to 8 | 1 | 1 | 1 | 2 | 2 | 3 | 4 |
| 8 to 9 | 1 | 1 | 1 | 1 | 1 | 2 | 3 |
| 9 to 10 | 1 | 1 | 1 | 1 | 1 | 2 | 2 |
| 10 to 11 | 1 | 1 | 1 | 1 | 1 | 1 | 2 |

**Schedule: Line Cooks**

| | *Sunday* | *Monday* | *Tuesday* | *Wednesday* | *Thursday* | *Friday* | *Saturday* |
|---|---|---|---|---|---|---|---|
| 3 to 4 | 2 | 2 | 2 | 2 | 2 | 2 | 2 |
| 4 to 5 | 2 | 2 | 2 | 2 | 2 | 2 | 2 |
| 5 to 6 | 2 | 2 | 2 | 2 | 2 | 3 | 3 |
| 6 to 7 | 2 | 2 | 2 | 2 | 3 | 3 | 4 |
| 7 to 8 | 2 | 2 | 2 | 2 | 3 | 3 | 4 |
| 8 to 9 | 2 | 2 | 2 | 2 | 2 | 3 | 3 |
| 9 to 10 | 2 | 2 | 2 | 2 | 2 | 2 | 3 |
| 10 to 11 | 2 | 2 | 2 | 2 | 2 | 2 | 2 |

These are not actual employee schedules but the exact number of food servers and line cooks needed to work each hour of the day and each day of the week.

As you can tell by looking at the above schedules, the number of employees needed varies by the hour of the dinner period. The best way to address this situation is to have multiple start times for employees to work. Some employees may be scheduled to begin work at 3:00 and others at 4:00 or even 5:00. The employees who begin their shift at 3:00 are the first employees to leave. Generally, the actual level of business determines what time these employees will clock out. This helps to eliminate the need for overtime.

If Anna's Annex were a nonunion operation, Anna could hire a combination of full- and part-time employees. The full-time employees can work less than 40 hours when business is slow. The part-time employees can work extra hours when business is good.

If Anna's Annex employed union members, Anna could use the staffing guide and the average customer forecast to determine the number of full-time employees to hire. If the above schedules are a fair representation of the average business per week, then Anna would hire one full-time server and two full-time line cooks. Steady extras would then be hired to work the remaining shifts. Of course, the full-time union employees would be scheduled for five shifts per week, eight hours per shift.

The last step in the scheduling process is to put employee names and start and stop times in the schedule form and to ensure that enough employees are scheduled to meet the demands of the customers. An employee schedule will look like this:

**Schedule: Dining Room Servers**

| | *Sunday* | *Monday* | *Tuesday* | *Wednesday* | *Thursday* | *Friday* | *Saturday* |
|---|---|---|---|---|---|---|---|
| Servers | | | | | | | |
| Tina | 3 to 11 | 3 to 11 | 3 to 11 | off | off | 3 to 11 | 3 to 11 |
| Kayli | | | | 3 to phase* | 3 to phase* | 5 to phase* | 5 to phase* |
| Mikayla | | | | 6 to 11 | 5 to 11 | 6 to phase* | 6 to phase* |
| Heather | | | | | | | 6 to phase* |

*Phase means that the level of business has slowed down enough for some staff to clock out.

**Schedule: Line Cooks**

| | *Sunday* | *Monday* | *Tuesday* | *Wednesday* | *Thursday* | *Friday* | *Saturday* |
|---|---|---|---|---|---|---|---|
| Raymond | 3 to11 | 3 to 11 | off | off | 3 to 11 | 3 to 11 | 3 to 11 |
| James | off | off | 3 to 11 | 3 to 11 | 3 to 11 | 3 to 11 | 3 to 11 |
| Dustin | off | 3 to 11 | 3 to 11 | 3 to 11 | 6 to phase | off | 5 to phase |
| Jeremy | 3 to 11 | | | | | 5 to phase | 6 to phase |

## EMPLOYEE PAYROLL CALCULATIONS

Employees are paid for the hours they work. The basic payroll calculation is:

Number of hours worked × the hourly pay rate = gross pay

Then the employer subtracts income tax (federal, state, and local), and Social Security tax from the employees' gross pay to arrive at the employees' net pay.

Raymond, one of our line cooks, earns $12.50 an hour. Raymond worked 30 hours last week. What is his gross pay?

30 (number of hours worked) × $12.50 (hourly pay rate)
= $375.00 gross pay

Raymond must pay federal and possibly state and local income taxes. For this example, federal, state, and local taxes are 18% (.18) of Raymond's gross income.

$ 375.00 (gross pay) × .18 (18% of gross)
= $67.50 amount of total income taxes

Raymond must also pay 7.5 percent (.075) of his gross wages for Social Security. Raymond's Social Security deduction is

$ 375.00 (gross pay) × .075 (7.5% of gross)
= $28.13 amount of Social Security deduction

Therefore, Raymond's gross income is reduced by $67.50 (income tax) and $28.13 (Social Security). What is his net pay?

$375.00 − ($67.50 + $28.13) = $375.00 − 95.63
= $279.37 net pay

Anna's Annex has additional expenses that must be paid by Anna as Raymond's employer. Anna is liable to pay the federal, state, and local governments the monies withheld from Raymond's paycheck (the tax amount of $67.50 and the Social Security amount of $28.13). In addition, Anna must pay 7.5 percent (.075) to the federal government's fund for Raymond's Social Security. Anna pays $28.13 to Social Security for Raymond.

Then Anna must pay a percentage of Raymond's gross to the federal (FUTA) and state (SUTA) government funds that covers an employee's unemployment and injured worker's compensation. For this example, the federal and state fund are 1 percent, respectively.

$$\$375.00 \text{ (Raymond's gross)} \times .01 \text{ (1\%)} = \$3.75$$

Anna pays $3.75 to the federal fund and $3.75 to the state fund. The total Anna pays to the fund for Raymond is

$$\$3.75 \text{ (1\% of Raymond's gross)} \times 2 \text{ (federal and state)} = \$7.50$$

Then it just so happens that Raymond is benefit eligible. The benefits that Raymond receives cost Anna an additional $3.00 for every hour that Raymond works. This $3.00 an hour is paid to the health-insurance company that provides coverage to Anna's employees.

30 (number of hours Raymond worked)
× $ 3.00 (amount per hour) = $90.00 for health insurance

Raymond's payroll is now complete:

| | *Gross Pay* | *Federal / State / Local Tax* | *Social Security* | *FUTA / SUTA* | *Benefits* |
|---|---|---|---|---|---|
| Raymond pays to government | $375.00 | $67.50 | $28.13 | $0.00 | |
| Anna pays to government for Raymond | | | $28.13 | $7.50 | |
| Anna pays for Raymond's benefits | | | | | $90.00 |
| Total Anna pays for Raymond's 30 hours worked | $375.00 | | $28.13 | $7.50 | $90.00 |
| Total Anna sends to governmental agencies | | $ 67.50 | $56.26 | $7.50 | |

| | |
|---|---|
| Raymond earned: | $375.00 |
| Anna's share of Social Security: | $28.13 |
| Anna's cost for FUTA and SUTA: | $7.50 |
| Anna's cost for insurance: | $90.00 |
| Total cost to Anna's Annex for Raymond: | $500.63 |

Anna is required by law to send Raymond's federal, state, and local taxes to the correct governmental agencies along with the combined Social Security payments and the FUTA and SUTA tax.

| | |
|---|---|
| Anna sends to the tax agencies: | $67.50 |
| Anna sends to Social Security: | $56.26 |
| Anna sends to FUTA and SUTA: | $7.50 |
| Total Anna must sent to government: | $131.26 |

Anna actually pays Raymond more than $12.50 per hour:

$500.63 (total cost for 30 hours) / 30 (hours) = $16.69 per hour

## TIP EARNERS

The Internal Revenue Service (IRS) has developed a system of taxation for employees who earn tips. Food servers, beverage servers, and bartenders are included under this system. The legislation is called the Tip Rate Determination Agreement (TRDA) or Tip Rate Alternative Commitment (TRAC). The TRDA or TRAC are basically agreements between a food service operation where employees earn tips and the IRS. The agreement states that each tipped employee earns a certain dollar amount of tips per hour worked. The total of the hourly wage and the tip income is then used to determine the employees' and the employer's tax liability.

At Anna's Annex the TRDA states that all of the food servers earn $7.50 an hour in tips. Anna pays her food servers $4.25 per hour. This is less than minimum wage. In some states it is legal to pay a tip earner less than the minimum wage because their tip income is considered a part of their hourly pay. In other states, tip earners must be paid the minimum wage.

The TRDA complicates the paycheck process for Anna as she calculates the paycheck for her food servers. Tina, a food server, worked 28 hours last week:

28 (number of hours worked) × $4.25 (hourly pay rate)
= $119.00 gross pay at $4.25 per hour

But Tina's federal, state, and local taxes, along with the Social Security payment and the FUTA and SUTA, are based on the $4.25 hourly rate plus the $7.50 an hour of tipped income.

$4.25 (hourly rate) + $7.50 (TRDA hourly rate)
= $11.75 per hour

Tina's federal, state, and local tax, along with Social Security payment and the FUTA and SUTA are based on $11.75 an hour, not $4.25 an hour:

28 (number of hours worked) × $11.75 (TRDA hourly rate)
= $329.00

Anna pays Social Security and FUTA and SUTA for Tina based on a $329.00 paycheck.

The hourly-rate employees are paid is a percentage of the total cost to the food service operator. The cost of labor can be the largest controllable expense in a food service operation. Due to this fact, the wise operator prepares a staffing guide and a weekly forecast before scheduling employees. This ensures that customers will be properly served and payroll will be controlled.

## LABOR COST AND CONTROL TECHNIQUES: REVIEW PROBLEMS

1. Why is it important to control the cost of labor?

2. What is a staffing guide?

3. What are the advantages to utilizing a staffing guide?

4. What is a forecast?

5. What is a schedule?

6. What are the advantages of forecasting prior to preparing the weekly schedule?

7. What is the basic formula for determining an employee's weekly pay?

8. What other components are included in the payroll calculations for employees?

9. Do employees actually earn more or less than their stated hourly wage? Why?

10. Staffing guide and schedule: Using the following information, create a staffing guide and a schedule for the dishwashers at a local university's student cafeteria.

    The cafeteria is open from 6 A.M. to 10 A.M. for breakfast, seven days a week. Five hundred students are eligible to eat in the cafeteria, but the average number of students for breakfast is 250. The breakdown is as follows:

| | |
|---|---|
| 6 to 7 A.M. | 25 students |
| 7 to 8 A.M. | 75 students |
| 8 to 9 A.M. | 100 students |
| 9 to 10 A.M. | 50 students |

The dishwashers wash both the pots and pans used for food prep and the serving dishes. The cafeteria needs 1 dishwasher per hour for every 25 students.

| Staffing Guide: Dishwashers | |
|---|---|
| | |
| | |
| | |
| | |
| | |
| | |
| | |
| | |
| | |
| | |
| | |

**Schedule: Dishwashers**

| | *Sunday* | *Monday* | *Tuesday* | *Wednesday* | *Thursday* | *Friday* | *Saturday* |
|---|---|---|---|---|---|---|---|
| | | | | | | | |
| | | | | | | | |
| | | | | | | | |
| | | | | | | | |

**11.** Payroll calculations: Tina is the waitress we discussed at the end of the chapter. She worked 28 hours last week and earns $4.25 an hour and has a TRDA of $7.50 an hour.

a. What is the gross on Tina's paycheck?

b. If the combined federal, state, and local tax rate is 21 percent, what is Tina's tax liability?

c. Social Security is taxed at a rate of 7.5 percent for the employee and the employer. What is the Social Security tax on Tina's earnings?

d. What is Tina's net income?

e. Anna pays FUTA and SUTA for Tina at a rate of 1.5 percent for each fund. What is the total cost of FUTA and SUTA to Anna?

f. What is the total cost per hour for Anna to have Tina as an employee?

### Labor Cost and Control Techniques Review Question Answers

1. It is important to control labor cost because it can be the highest controllable expense for a food service operation. It can average between 30 and 40 cents per sales dollar.
2. A staffing guide is a graph or chart that states the number of employees needed for different levels of business / number of customers.
3. The advantages of using a staffing guide is it helps to plan and control labor costs.
4. A forecast is an estimate of the number of customers that will visit our restaurant per meal period.
5. A schedule is a list of employees and the hours they are asked to work.
6. Forecasting prior to scheduling ensures that we have the proper number of employees scheduled to take care of our guests.
7. The basic formula for determining an employees weekly pay is:

   Number of hours worked × hourly pay rate

8. Other computations included in an employee's payroll calculation is federal, state, and local taxes, and Social Security.
9. Employees earn more than the hourly wage they receive. The employer has to pay half of the employee's Social Security, FUTA and SUTA, and possibly all or some of the cost of benefits.

**Staffing Guide: Dishwashers**

| *Number of Students* | *Number of Dishwashers* |
|---|---|
| 25 | 1 |
| 50 | 2 |
| 75 | 3 |
| 100 | 4 |
| 125 | 5 |
| 150 | 6 |
| 175 | 7 |
| 200 | 8 |
| 225 | 9 |
| 250 | 10 |

**Schedule: Dishwashers**

| | *Sunday* | *Monday* | *Tuesday* | *Wednesday* | *Thursday* | *Friday* | *Saturday* |
|---|---|---|---|---|---|---|---|
| 6 to 7 | 1 | 1 | 1 | 1 | 1 | 1 | 1 |
| 7 to 8 | 3 | 3 | 3 | 3 | 3 | 3 | 3 |
| 8 to 9 | 4 | 4 | 4 | 4 | 4 | 4 | 4 |
| 9 to 10 | 2 | 2 | 2 | 2 | 2 | 2 | 2 |

**10.** Staffing guide and schedule
**11.** Payroll calculations

a. Tina's gross is

$4.25 (hourly rate) × 28 (hours worked) = $119.00

b. The combined taxes must be calculated on Tina's hourly wage and TRDA hourly rate. Therefore, the tax rate is on:

$4.25 an hour + $7.50 an hour = $11.75 per hour

$11.75 (an hour) × 28 (hours)
= $329.00 gross for tax purposes

Then:

$329.00 (gross for tax purposes) × .21 (tax rate)
= $69.09 total tax

c. \$329.00 (gross for tax purposes) × .075 (Social Security rate) = \$24.68 Social Security tax Tina and Anna both pay this amount.

d. Tina's net income is

\$119.00 − (\$69.09 + \$24.68) = \$119.00 − \$93.77 = \$25.23

e. FUTA and SUTA are each 1.5% of \$329.00

\$329.00 × .015 (1.5%)
= \$4.94 for FUTA and \$4.94 for SUTA

f. Anna's total cost for Tina is:

| | |
|---|---|
| Paycheck: | \$119.00 |
| Social Security: | \$24.68 |
| FUTA | \$4.94 |
| SUTA | \$4.94 |
| Total | \$153.56 |

Hourly rate is \$ 153.56 / 28 (hours) = \$5.48.

# Chapter 9

# SIMPLIFIED MATHEMATICS AND COMPUTERS IN FOOD SERVICE

Are there some tricks of the trade to help keep all of the math knowledge at the tips of our fingers? Are there systems that are used to help us keep track of all the information that we need to know? Is there an easier way?

The *Levinson approach,* named for Charles Levinson, and discussed in the fifth edition of *Purchasing* by John Stefanelli and Andrew Feinstein, is an easier way to compare different products before making the purchasing decision. This approach also makes it easier to cost a portion of an item, a plate, or an entire meal. The reason the Levinson approach is easier is because it develops a mathematical constant for each item we serve.

## PORTION FACTORS AND PORTION DIVIDERS

A mathematical constant is the same concept as the multipliers discussed in Chapter 2, "Units of Measure." The constant developed by the Levinson approach is an "integer and/or a mixed number" that represents a product's portion size and its yield percentage. This constant is called a *portion divider.* Every item on the menu has its own portion divider. Once the portion divider is developed for each item, it assists us with purchasing and costing decisions.

However, before we can development the portion divider we must develop a *portion factor*. The portion factor is a term used to describe the number of portions served per AP units. Each item will have its own unique portion factor.

The formula for a portion factor is:

Unit of purchase / Portion size = Portion factor

Bone in, prime rib roasts are purchased by the pound. If we serve a 12-ounce portion of prime rib, our portion factor is

16 (ounces per pound) / 12 (ounces) = 1.33 (portion factor)

If we serve an 8-ounce portion of prime rib, our portion factor is

16 (ounces per pound) / 8 (ounces) = 2 (portion factor)

If we serve a 6-ounce portion of prime rib, our portion factor is:

16 (ounces per pound) / 6 (ounces) = 2.67 (portion factor)

As the prime rib example illustrates, if we offer a different size portion of the same item, each portion size has its own portion factor. Each item will have a unique portion divider, too.

The portion divider, as stated previously, is an integer and/or mixed number that describes the relationship between a product's portion size and the product's yield percentage. The portion divider is a mathematical constant that describes the product as an EP or AS (edible portion/as served) unit.

The formula for a portion divided is

Portion factor × Yield percentage = Portion divider

The yield percentage on the bone-in prime rib roast is 50 percent. What is the portion divider for the different size portions?

For the 12-ounce portion of prime rib, the portion divider is

1.33 (portion factor) × .50 (yield percentage)
= .665 (portion divider)

For the 8-ounce portion of prime rib, the portion divider is

2 (portion factor) × .50 (yield percentage) = 1 (portion divider)

For the 6-ounce portion of prime rib, the portion divider is

2.67 (portion factor) × .50 (yield percentage)
= 1.335 (portion divider)

We are catering a prime rib dinner for 250 guests. We purchase the bone-in prime rib roast for $2.00 per pound. Using the portion factors and portion dividers we developed for the different prime rib portion sizes, see how easy it is to develop an AP quantity, and the EP/AS cost of the prime rib portion.

| *Item* | *Prime Rib* | | |
|---|---|---|---|
| Unit of Purchase (U of P) | Pound | | |
| Portion Size (PS) | 12 oz. | 8 oz. | 6 oz. |
| Portion Factor (PF): U of P / PS = PF | 1.33 | 2 | 2.67 |
| Yield Percentage (Y%) | .50 | .50 | .50 |
| Portion Divider (PD): PF × Y % = PD | .665 | 1 | 1.335 |
| Purchase Price per Unit (PU) | $2.00 | $2.00 | $2.00 |
| Portion Cost (PC): PU / PD = PC | $3.00 | $2.00 | $1.50 |
| Number of Covers (# Covers) | 250 | 250 | 250 |
| AP Weight: # Covers / PD = AP Wt. | 376# | 250# | 187# |
| Total Cost per Portion | $3.00 | $2.00 | $1.50 |

Using the Levinson approach, we can evaluate the AP weight and the portion cost for the same item with different portion sizes. This approach gives us AP quantity and portion cost using the portion divider.

This approach can also be used to compare similar products that have a different yield percentage. An oven-ready prime rib roast has an 80 percent yield and costs $2.95 per pound. A bone-in prime rib roast has a 50 percent yield and costs $2.00 per pound. The portion size is 8 ounces. Which is the best buy?

The portion factor for the oven-ready prime rib is

16 (ounces per pound) / 8 (portion size) = 2

The portion divider for the oven-ready prime rib is

2 (portion factor) × .80 (yield percentage) = 1.60

The cost per portion for the oven-ready prime rib is

$2.95 (purchase price per unit) / 1.60 (portion divider)
= $1.84 per portion

The cost per portion for the oven-ready prime rib roast is $1.84.

The cost per portion from the bone-in Prime Rib (from the chart) is $2.00.

The best buy is the oven-ready prime rib roast for $2.95 per pound.

This approach can be used regardless of the AP unit. Our catering department has just called to tell us they have sold the following menu for 40 guests this Friday. The food needs to be purchased ASAP, and they need a menu price. This is easy using the Levinson approach.

The spreadsheet in Table 9.1 on the next page lays out the process for developing a portion factor and a portion divider. The result of using this format is the correct amount of food to purchase and the correct cost per guest to serve the following banquet menu.

## BANQUET MENU PURCHASING, PRICING, AND YIELD INFORMATION

Shrimp: 26/30 per pound, $6.00 per pound, portion size 6 each
Soup a la Banquet: recipe yield 2 gallons, recipe cost $8.00, portion size 6 oz.

Sorbet: $3.00 per quart, portion size 2 # 60 scoops
Steak: $4.50 per pound, 8 oz. portion-control product
Green beans: $0.98 per pound, yield 75%, portion size 2 oz.
Chocolate cake: $10.00 per cake, yield 8 slices

**TABLE 9.1**

Simplified Cost Control Worksheet

| Item | Unit of Purchase U of P | Portion Size PS | Portion Factor PF U of P/PS = PF | Yield % (Y %) | Portion Divider PD PF × Y% = PD | Price/Unit (PU) | Portion Cost PC PU/PD = PC | Number of Covers (# Covers) | AP Weight to Purchase # Covers/ PD = AP Wt. | Total Cost Per Cover |
|---|---|---|---|---|---|---|---|---|---|---|
| Shrimp | 26/30 each | 6 | 28/6 = 4.67 | 100% | 4.67 × 1.00 = 4.67 | $6.00 | $6.00/4.67 = $1.28 | 40 | 40/4.67 = 8.56 # | $1.28 |
| Soup | 256 oz | 6 oz | 256/6 = 42.67 | 100% | 42.67 × 1.00 = 42.67 | $8.00 | $8.00/42.67 = $0.19 | 40 | 40/42.67 = .94 recipe | $0.19 |
| Sorbet | Quart | 2#60 | 32/1.07 = 30 | 100% | 30 × 1.00 = 30 | $3.00 | $3.00/30 = $0.10 | 40 | 40/30 = 1.33 | $0.10 |
| Steak | 16 ounces | 8 oz | 16/8 = 2 | 100% | 2 × 1.00 = 2 | $4.50 | $4.50/2 = $2.25 | 40 | 40/2 = 20 # | $2.25 |
| Beans | 16 ounces | 2 oz | 16/2 = 8 | 75% | 8 × .75 = 6 | $0.98 | $0.98/6 = $0.163 | 40 | 40/6 = 6.67 # | $0.16 |
| Cake | 8 slices | 1 | 8/1 = 8 | 100% | 8 × 1.00 = 8 | $10.00 | $10.00/8 = $1.25 | 40 | 40/8 = 5 cakes | $1.25 |
| | | | | | | | | | Total Cost per Cover | $5.23 |

## SIMPLIFIED MATHEMATICS: REVIEW PROBLEMS

1. What is the formula for a portion factor?

2. What is the formula for a portion divider?

3. We serve a 5-ounce portion of taco meat. We have the option of purchasing taco meat for $3.25 a pound with an 87 percent yield or taco meat for $2.25 a pound with a 67 percent yield.

   a. Which product offers us better value?

   b. If the price per pound changes from $3.25 to $3.49 and from $2.25 to $2.75, which product now offers us better value?

4. The food and beverage director has decided to have a set menu in the restaurant for Easter Sunday dinner. The forecast is 300 covers. The menu is:

   Pork tenderloin: $3.95 per pound, 87% yield, 6-ounce portion
   Broccoli: $1.29 pound, 63% yield, 4-ounce portion size
   Baked potato: 8.00 per case of 80 each, portion size is 1 each
   Peach pie: $4.00 per pie, yield 8 slices, portion size 1 slice

   Using Table 9.2 on the next page, how much product do we need to purchase and how much does one cover cost?

### Simplified Mathematics: Review Answers

1. Unit of purchase / portion size = portion factor
2. Portion factor × yield % = portion divider
3. a. 5-ounce portion, $3.25 per pound, 87% yield
   16 / 5 = 3.2 (PF), 3.2 × .87 = 2.78 (PD), $3.25 / 2.78 = $1.17 portion cost
   5-ounce portion, $2.25 per pound, 67% yield
   16 / 5 = 3.2 (PF), 3.2 × .67 = 2.14 (PD), $2.25 / 2.14 = $1.05 portion cost
   The $2.25 product offers us better value.
   b. $3.49 / 2.78 = $1.26 new portion cost
   $2.75 / 2.14 = $1.29 new portion cost
   The $3.49 product offers us better value.
4. See Table 9.3

**TABLE 9.2**

Simplified Cost Control Worksheet

| *Item* | *Unit of Purchase U of P* | *Portion Size PS* | *Portion Factor PF U of P/PS = PF* | *Yield % (Y %)* | *Portion Divider PD PF × Y% = PD* | *Price/Unit (PU)* | *Portion Cost PC PU/PD = PC* | *Number of Covers (# Covers)* | *AP Weight to Purchase # Covers/ PD = AP Wt.* | *Total Cost Per Cover* |
|---|---|---|---|---|---|---|---|---|---|---|
| | | | | | | | | | | |
| | | | | | | | | | | |
| | | | | | | | | | | |
| | | | | | | | | | | |
| | | | | | | | | | | |
| | | | | | | | | | | |
| | | | | | | | | | | |
| | | | | | | | | | | |
| | | | | | | | | | | |
| | | | | | | | | | | |
| | | | | | | | | | | |
| | | | | | | | | | | |
| | | | | | | | | | | |
| | | | | | | | | | | |
| | | | | | | | | | | |
| | | | | | | | | | | |
| | | | | | | | | | | |
| | | | | | | | | | | |
| | | | | | | | | | | |
| | | | | | | | | | | |
| | | | | | | | | | | |
| | | | | | | | | | | |
| | | | | | | | | | | |
| | | | | | | | | | | |
| | | | | | | | | | | |

**TABLE 9.3**

Simplified Cost Control Worksheet Review Answers

| Item | Unit of Purchase U of P | Portion Size PS | Portion Factor PF U of P/PS = PF | Yield % (Y %) | Portion Divider PD PF × Y% = PD | Price/Unit (PU) | Portion Cost PC PU/PD = PC | Number of Covers (# Covers) | AP Weight to Purchase # Covers/ PD = AP Wt. | Total Cost Per Cover |
|---|---|---|---|---|---|---|---|---|---|---|
| Pork | 16 oz. | 6 oz | 16/6 = 2.67 | 87% | 2.67 × .87 = 2.32 | $3.95 | $3.95/2.32 = $1.70 | 300 | 300/2.32 = 129.3 # | $1.70 |
| | | | | | | | | | | |
| Broccoli | 16 oz | 4 oz | 16/4 = 4 | 63% | 4 × .63 = 2.52 | $1.29 | $1.29/2.52 = $0.51 | 300 | 300/2.52 = 119 # | $0.51 |
| | | | | | | | | | | |
| Potato | 80 each | 1 each | 80/1 = 80 | 100% | 80 × 1.00 = 80 | $8.00 | $8.00/80 = $0.10 | 300 | 300/80 = 3.75 cs | $0.10 |
| | | | | | | | | | | |
| Pie | 8 each | 1 each | 8/1 = 8 | 100% | 8 × 1.00 = 8 | $4.00 | $4.00/8 = $0.50 | 300 | 300/8 = 37.5 pies | $0.50 |
| | | | | | | | | | | |
| | | | | | | | | | Portion cost | $2.81 |

## COMPUTERS IN FOOD SERVICE: SMALL RESTAURANTS AND PERSONAL COMPUTERS (PC)

A PC has the capacity to assist us in many ways with the storage, retrieval, and mathematical calculations for all of our food service needs. Anyone can sit down at a personal computer (PC) and develop a "system" that will deliver the information that is needed for each operation. A small independent operator can invest in a PC. It can be used to keep track of purveyors and price lists for purchasing. It can be used to track inventory, including par levels, usage, and cost.

A PC can be used to cost out a recipe and accurately increase or decrease the yield. It can determine the yield of an item as it changes from AP to EP to AS. It can be used to forecast production based on sales of each item from your guest history. A spreadsheet, like the one used to cost out the banquet menus, can perform the calculations for a portion factor and a portion divider. A good printer can print menus in a much more cost-effective manner than the neighborhood print shop. Computer skills can prove to be a great asset to a food service operator.

### Food Service Operations and PC-Based Software

Commercial software packages are sometimes cost-effective. The most popular PC-based software package for purchasing, inventory control, and recipe costing is Chef Tec. The Chef Tec software package stores purchasing and inventory data as well as unit pricing information. At the end of the month the pricing data are available for the preparation of monthly financial statements.

The pricing data are also used to cost out a recipe. As the list of ingredients and their quantity are put into the recipe format, the current price per unit in inventory is attached to the product in the recipe. It works very well as long as the purchasing units of measure match the recipe units of measure. If the yield on a recipe is changed, the software automatically adjusts the ingredient quantities.

### AS 400-Based Computerized Inventory Purchasing Software

A PC-based system cannot accommodate a full-service hotel with multiple food and beverage outlets or a large commercial or noncommercial operation. These types of operations need to have many employees access the system simultaneously. These operations commonly use an AS 400 hardware unit and a fairly sophisticated inventory purchasing software package.

The software commonly used is The Stratton Warren LLC Inventory and Purchasing Software Package. This system is designed specifically to meet the needs of the food service industry. This system is used to place orders, to receive orders, and to maintain a perpetual inventory. It is used to requisition food from the storage areas to the production areas, and it transfers the cost of food from the inventory account to the food service outlet/production unit.

It tracks inventory par levels so we know when we are running low on products and an order can be placed. The package is capable of printing out a report on a wide variety of topics, from a perpetual inventory list to an inventory usage by item or by food service outlet. It can cost out recipes and transfer items and costs for one restaurant to another. It can even track labor costs.

Technology is a part of our lives, and it can assist us with all of our mathematical needs.

# Appendix I
# USING A CALCULATOR

A calculator is an electronic device that accurately performs mathematical operations. Calculators are available in a variety of price ranges, and some can perform fairly sophisticated mathematical operations and functions. A basic calculator is all that is necessary to perform the mathematics for the culinary arts. Accuracy is assured when the correct numbers are entered in the correct sequence. This is especially important with subtraction and division. If the numbers for these functions are entered in reverse order, the answer will not be correct.

## ADDITION WITH A CALCULATOR

Addition with a calculator is a simple process. The first number is entered in the calculator and is displayed. Then the plus (+) sign is entered. The second number is entered and is displayed. Then the equals (=) sign is entered and the sum of the numbers is displayed.

$$10 + 10 = 20$$

## SUBTRACTION WITH A CALCULATOR

Subtraction is also a simple process. The first number is entered and is displayed. Then the minus (−) sign is entered. Then the second number is entered and is displayed. Then the equals (=) sign is entered and the answer appears in the display.

$$20 - 10 = 10$$

## MULTIPLICATION WITH A CALCULATOR

Multiplication is accomplished by entering the first number in the calculator and having the number displayed. Then the times (×) sign is entered. The second number is entered and it is displayed. Then the equals (=) sign is entered and the product is displayed.

$$10 \times 2 + 20$$

## DIVISION WITH A CALCULATOR

Division can be presented in different formats. Division can be presented as a fraction, which is a numerator over a denominator. In this format, the numerator quantity is entered into the calculator first and it is displayed. Then the division (÷) sign is entered. Next the denominator quantity is entered and it is displayed. Then the equals (=) sign is entered and the quotient is displayed.

If the fraction is $\frac{3}{4}$, the sequence is $3 \div 4 = .75$

Division can also be presented as a divisor divided into a dividend: *divisor* $\overline{)\textit{dividend}}$. In this format, the dividend is entered into the calculator first and is displayed. Then the division (÷) key is entered. Next the divisor is entered into the calculator and is displayed. Then the equals (=) sign is entered and the quotient is displayed.

If the problem is presented in this format, $4\,\overline{)3}$, the sequence is: $3 \div 4 = .75$

## DECIMALS WITH A CALCULATOR

Mathematical operations with decimals are the same as has been mentioned above, with one exception. Whenever there is a decimal point in a quantity, the decimal point must be entered into the calculator. If the decimal point has been entered correctly, the answer in the display will place the decimal point in the correct place. If the decimal point has not been entered correctly into the calculator, the answer in the display will not be correct.

## PERCENTAGES WITH A CALCULATOR

A quantity with a percent sign is the equivalent as the same quantity with a decimal. For example:

$$50\% = .50$$

Mathematical operations with percentages can be performed with a calculator. However, the answer in the display will contain a decimal point and not a percent sign. If you multiply a number by a quantity represented as a percentage, the procedure is as follows. The number is entered and is displayed. Then the times (×) sign is entered. Then the percent is entered as a quantity and then the percent key is entered. The answer is displayed as a decimal.

If the problem is 5 × 50%, the sequence is 5 × 50% = 2.5. The decimal point is inserted at the correct place.

Some prefer to use the percent key in this situation, while some are more comfortable changing the percent to a decimal and then performing the mathematical operation. Either way yields the same answer.

## USING A CALCULATOR: REVIEW PROBLEMS

Add the following numbers.

**1.** $17 + 17 =$

**2.** $13 + 20 =$

**3.** $6 + 22 =$

Subtract the following numbers.

**4.** $16 - 12 =$

**5.** $45 - 9 =$

**6.** $32 - 18 =$

Multiply the following numbers.

**7.** $21 \times 21 =$

**8.** $16 \times 4 =$

**9.** $22 \times 1 =$

Divide the following quantities.

**10.** $\frac{6}{10} =$

**11.** $\frac{7}{12} =$

**12.** $6\overline{)10} =$

## Using a Calculator: Review Answers

1. 34
2. 33
3. 28
4. 4
5. 36
6. 14
7. 441
8. 64
9. 22
10. .60
11. .58
12. 1.667

# Appendix II
# COMMON ITEM YIELDS

| *Product* | *Yield Percentage* |
|---|---|
| Meat: | |
| Prime rib roast (109) | .50, or 50% |
| Chicken: | |
| Large fryer (clean meat) | .48, or 48% |
| Breast, whole, both halves | .296, or 29.6% |
| Wings, whole | .107, or 10.7% |
| Legs, whole, drum and thigh | .276, or 27.6% |
| Seafood: Finfish | |
| Flounder, drawn to fillet | .45, or 45% |
| Vegetables: | |
| Broccoli, bunch whole | .628, or 62.8% |
| Carrots, whole jumbo | .836, or 83.6% |
| Celery, bunch | .688, or 68.8% |
| Lettuce, iceberg | .731, or 73.1% |
| Onion, bulb | .906, or 90.6% |
| Fruit: | |
| Apples | .85, or 85% |
| Melon, cantaloupe | .581, or 58.1% |
| Oranges, navel | .625, or 62.5% |
| Strawberries | .919, or 91.9% |

| *Product* | *Yield Percentage* |
|---|---|
| Legumes: | |
| Pinto beans, dry | 2.83, or 283% |
| Rice | |
| White, medium grain | 3.03, or 303% |

Courtesy of Francis T. Lynch, *The Book of Yields: Food Facts for Accurate Recipe Costing* (Hoboken, New Jersey: John Wiley & Sons, Inc., 2000).

# Appendix III
# CONVERSION TABLES

**Decimal Weight Equivalents**

| *Ounces* | | *Pounds* | *Ounces* | | *Pounds* |
|---|---|---|---|---|---|
| 1 oz. | = | 0.06 lb. | 16 oz. | = | 1.00 lb. |
| 2 oz. | = | 0.12 lb. | 32 oz. | = | 2.00 lb. |
| 3 oz. | = | 0.19 lb. | 35 oz. | = | 2.19 lb. |
| 4 oz. | = | 0.25 lb. | 48 oz. | = | 3.00 lb. |
| 5 oz. | = | 0.31 lb. | 64 oz. | = | 4.00 lb. |
| 6 oz. | = | 0.38 lb. | 71 oz. | = | 4.44 lb. |
| 7 oz. | = | 0.44 lb. | 80 oz. | = | 5.00 lb. |
| 8 oz. | = | 0.50 lb. | 96 oz. | = | 6.00 lb. |
| 9 oz. | = | 0.56 lb. | 106 oz. | = | 6.63 lb. |
| 10 oz. | = | 0.62 lb. | 112 oz. | = | 7.00 lb. |
| 11 oz. | = | 0.69 lb. | 128 oz. | = | 8.00 lb. |
| 12 oz. | = | 0.75 lb. | 141 oz. | = | 8.82 lb. |
| 13 oz. | = | 0.81 lb. | 144 oz. | = | 9.00 lb. |
| 14 oz. | = | 0.88 lb. | 160 oz. | = | 10.00 lb. |
| 15 oz. | = | 0.94 lb. | | | |

### Decimal Equivalents for Fractions of a Unit

Whole units are on the left. The fraction of part of the unit is to the right.

| If the whole units are: | the decimal equivalents are part of: |
|---|---|
| ounces | 1 pound |
| tablespoons | 1 cup |
| cups | 1 gallon |

| Fraction of Part of the Unit | | | | | | |
|---|---|---|---|---|---|---|
| *Number of Units* | | *+ 1/4 of unit* | *+ 1/3 of unit* | *+ 1/2 of unit* | *+ 2/3 of unit* | *+ 3/4 of unit* |
| 0 | — | 0.02 | 0.02 | 0.03 | 0.04 | 0.05 |
| 1 | 0.06 | .08 | .08 | .09 | .10 | .11 |
| 2 | .12 | .14 | .15 | .16 | .17 | .17 |
| 3 | .19 | .20 | .21 | .22 | .23 | .23 |
| 4 | .25 | .27 | .27 | .28 | .29 | .30 |
| 5 | .31 | .33 | .33 | .34 | .35 | .36 |
| 6 | .38 | .39 | .40 | .41 | .42 | .42 |
| 7 | .44 | .45 | .46 | .47 | .48 | .48 |
| 8 | .50 | .52 | .52 | .53 | .54 | .55 |
| 9 | .56 | .58 | .58 | .59 | .60 | .61 |
| 10 | .62 | .64 | .65 | .66 | .67 | .67 |
| 11 | .69 | .70 | .71 | .72 | .73 | .73 |
| 12 | .75 | .77 | .77 | .78 | .79 | .80 |
| 13 | .81 | .83 | .83 | .84 | .85 | .86 |
| 14 | .88 | .89 | .90 | .91 | .92 | .92 |
| 15 | .94 | .95 | .96 | .97 | .98 | .98 |
| 16 | 1.00 | 1.02 | 1.02 | 1.03 | 1.04 | 1.05 |

| Metric Equivalents by Weight | |
|---|---|
| *U.S. Unit (fluid ounces)* | *Metric Unit* |
| Ounces (oz.) | Grams (g) |
| 1 ounce | 28.35 g |
| 4 ounces | 113.4 g |
| 8 ounces | 226.8 g |
| 16 ounces | 453.6 g |
| Pounds (lb.) | Grams (g) |
| 1 pound | 453.6 g |
| 2 pounds | 907.2 g |
| 2.2 pounds | 1,000 g (1 kilogram) |

| Metric Equivalents by Volume | |
|---|---|
| *U.S. Unit (fluid ounces)* | *Metric Unit* |
| 1 cup (8 fl oz) | 236.59 milliliters (mL) |
| 1 quart (32 fl oz) | 946.36 milliliters (mL) |
| 1.5 quarts (48 fl oz) | 1.42 liter (L) |
| 33.818 fl oz | 1.0 liter (L) |

| Volume Equivalents for Liquids | | |
|---|---|---|
| 1 tablespoon | = 3 teaspoons | = 0.5 fluid ounces |
| 1/8 cup | = 2 tablespoons | = 1 fluid ounce |
| 1/4 cup | = 4 tablespoons | = 2 fluid ounces |
| 1/3 cup | = 5 1/3 tablespoons | = 2.65 fluid ounces |
| 3/8 cup | = 6 tablespoons | = 3 fluid ounces |
| 1/2 cup | = 8 tablespoons | = 4 fluid ounces |
| 5/8 cup | = 10 tablespoons | = 5 fluid ounces |
| 2/3 cup | = 10 2/3 tablespoons | = 5.3 fluid ounces |
| 3/4 cup | = 12 tablespoons | = 6 fluid ounces |
| 7/8 cup | = 14 tablespoons | = 7 fluid ounces |
| 1 cup | = 16 tablespoons | = 8 fluid ounces |
| 1/2 pint | = 1 cup | = 8 fluid ounces |
| 1 pint | = 2 cups | = 16 fluid ounces |
| 1 quart | = 2 pints | = 32 fluid ounces |
| 1 gallon | = 4 quarts | = 128 fluid ounces |
| 1 peck | = 8 quarts (dry) | |
| 1 bushel | = 4 pecks | |

**Sizes and Capacities of Ladles**

| *Number on Ladle* | *Approximate Measure* |
|---|---|
| 1 ounce | 1/8 cup |
| 2 ounces | 1/4 cup |
| 4 ounces | 1/2 cup |
| 6 ounces | 3/4 cup |
| 8 ounces | 1 cup |
| 12 ounces | 1 1/2 cups |

| Sizes and Capacities of Scoops (Dishers) | |
|---|---|
| *Number on Scoop (Disher)* | *Level Measure* |
| 6 | ⅔ cup |
| 8 | ½ cup |
| 10 | ⅜ cup |
| 12 | ⅓ cup |
| 16 | ¼ cup |
| 20 | 3⅓ tablespoons |
| 24 | 2⅔ tablespoons |
| 30 | 2 tablespoons |
| 40 | 1⅔ tablespoons |
| 50 | 3¾ teaspoons |
| 60 | 3¼ teaspoons |
| 70 | 2¾ teaspoons |
| 100 | 2 teaspoons |

| Sizes and Capacities of Measuring/Serving Spoons | |
|---|---|
| *Size of Measuring/ Serving Spoon* | *Approximate Measure* |
| 2 ounces | ¼ cup |
| 3 ounces | ⅜ cup |
| 4 ounces | ½ cup |
| 6 ounces | ¾ cup |
| 8 ounces | 1 cup |

# GLOSSARY

**Average guest check** The amount of money the average guest spends on a meal in a restaurant. There will be a different average guest check for each meal period.

**Cash flow** The actual amount of cash that comes into and goes out of a food service operation.

**Common factor** A number that can be divided evenly into both the numerator and the denominator (of a fraction).

**Cost of sale** The actual dollar cost of food and/or beverage served to the guest.

**Decimal** A linear array of integers that represent a fraction.

**Directs** Food and/or beverage items that are received and go directly into meal production.

**Entree** Main course of a meal.

**Factor** One or more quantities that divides a given quantity without a remainder.

**Fraction** A quotient of two quantities shown as a numerator over a denominator.

**Gross profit** Profit after the cost of sale is subtracted from sales revenue.

**Improper fraction** A fraction whose numerator is equal to or greater than the denominator.

**Integer** A member of the set of positive or negative whole numbers and zero.

**Inventory** Products such as food, beverage, and supplies that are in storage and available for use in a food service operation.

**Least common denominator** The smallest number that can be divided evenly by two or more fractions' denominators.

**Least common multiple** The smallest quantity exactly divisible by two or more given quantities. The smallest number that is a multiple of two or more numbers.

**Lowest common denominator** See Least common denominator

**Mixed number** The sum of a whole number greater than zero and a proper fraction.

**Multiple** A quantity that can be divided into a number without a remainder.

**Multiplier** A quantity by which another number is multiplied.

**Noninteger number** A quantity that is not a whole number.

**Percentage** The amount or rate per one hundred.

**Portion factor** An integer or mixed number that is calculated by dividing an item's unit of purchase by its portion size.

**Portion divider** An integer or mixed number that is calculated by multiplying an item's portion factor by its yield percentage.

**Prime number** A whole number that has itself and 1 as its only factors.

**Product** The number obtained by multiplying one quantity by another.

**Proper fraction** A fraction whose numerator is less than the denominator.

**Quotient** The number obtained by dividing one quantity by another.

**Reciprocal** Either of a pair of numbers whose product is 1; 1/4 and 4/1 are reciprocals.

**Whole number** An integer.

# INDEX